Life as a Student
A Christian's Guide to the Student's World

Samuel F. Koroma

Kingdom Publishers

Life as a Student
Copyright © Samuel F. Koroma

All rights reserved. No part of this book may be reproduced in any form by photocopying or any electronic or mechanical means, including information storage or retrieval systems, without permission in writing from both the copyright owner and the publisher of the book. The right of Samuel F. Koroma to be identified as the author of this work has been asserted by him in accordance with the Copyright, Designs and Patents Act 1988 and any subsequent amendments thereto.
A catalogue record for this book is available from the British Library.

ISBN: 978-1-913247-12-6

1st Edition by Kingdom Publishers
Kingdom Publishers
London, UK.

DEDICATION

This book is dedicated to my mother Mrs. Cecilia Nyangbe Koroma, based in Texas, U.S.A, my wife Mrs. Madiana Nyamu Koroma, my two lovely daughters – Neriah Nyande Koroma and Cecilia Nyangbe Koroma II, all members of the Koroma family and my posterity. This book is also dedicated to the Student-domain, globally, and I pray that the information contained, would help walk them into their academic destinies – in the Name of Jesus Christ.

I pray that the Almighty God would glorify Himself in the life of everyone who reads this book – in the Name of Jesus Christ.

ACKNOWLEDGEMENT

'And the LORD spake unto Moses, saying, see, I have called by name Bezaleel the son of Uri, the son of Hur, of the tribe of Judah: And I have filled him with the Spirit of God, in wisdom, and in understanding, and in knowledge, and in all manner of workmanship, to devise cunning works, to work in gold, and in silver, and in brass, And in cutting of stones, to set them, and in carving of Timber, to work in all manner of workmanship.' - Exodus 31:1-5

Wisdom, Knowledge and Understanding emanate from God. If I am able to successfully complete this project, then it's all because of the empowerment from The Almighty God. And for that reason, I offer the greatest gratitude to The Almighty God. I warmly appreciate my Chief Critic Mrs. Khai Moriba, based in the United States of America, for her advanced analytical skill, strong adjudication and confidentiality. I also thank my first Critic, Abraham Maada Tucker, the first person to see the draft of this book, who inspired me to continue. I thank all members of the Koroma family, especially my sisters Mrs. Sabiatu Harry-James, who internationally coordinated all activities of this project, and Mrs. Suba S. Vincent, who successfully executed the banking transaction in the United Kingdom. To my nephew John Kall Vandi, who recommended Kingdom Publishers, I say thank you, thank you and thank you. Ineffable thanks to my sister Mrs. Kadi Gembeh, who financially supported, and inspired, me right through my University education, and also supported me in this project. I also thank Kadi's husband, Dr. Solomon Gembeh, for being a human guide to her.

The Almighty God would immeasurably bless all of you who supported me in varied ways – in the Name of Jesus Christ.

PREFACE

Life as a Student is about my personal experiences, especially at the University, and I employed those empirical facts to help Students overcome educational obstacles. It's not just a read-and-study guidebook, but the inception of a planetary lifetime campaign, which serves to guard prospective Students, Graduates, University Authorities and others interested in academic activities.

In spite of its partial secularity, **Life as a Student** was poured into my heart, by The Heavenly Father, as I approached the terminal point of my Engineering Bachelor Course. Some of the incidents mentioned might be considered irrelevant, but these would be justified as you walk through my elucidation. I did not add flamboyant colours to my personality, but revealed existing potential, which helps you recognize the transformation and see how individuals can be manipulated. The declarations made are real and I strongly admonish you to accept them as presented.

In life, different individuals possess different talents. For this reason, different Personalities have different desires. Someone can have a dream to be an Engineer, and another a Lawyer, but transforming that fantasy into reality depends on a number of factors hidden in **Life as a Student**. Probably, you are prepared to accept whatever life offers. But after crawling through this tome, you would realize that sometimes what life offers is nothing more than a minute distorted compensation.

Graduating from Fourah Bay College, University of Sierra Leone, was more of an optical illusion than a reality. Intelligent Students step into the University and, with hard work, succeed within the required frame of time. I am intelligent, but my level of intelligence did not clearly show up, especially at the concluding stage of my undergraduate education. The road to my certification was more than rocky, for in the intellectual fight, I was always on the defensive. At some point, I almost declined. But with the help of our Lord Jesus Christ, I maintained a sense of tenacity. Frustration was underway, but with the assistance of my relations at home and abroad, I maintained a good state of fortitude.

Some believe you must accept responsibility for every difficulty faced in life, but I believe you only take up the blame when you clearly understand the protocol to true success - when you know how to genuinely succeed and how to truly fail. **Life as a Student** would make the ways to delay, failure and success comprehensible. Then when you delay, when you fail, when you succeed, you have no alternative but to hold yourself responsible.

So diligently read through this guidebook, identify the troubles, scrutinize your life, make rectifications where necessary and become an asset to humanity. Acknowledge your purpose of being at the University and enjoy a truly successful life as a Student.

CONTENTS

Dedication		5
Acknowledgement		7
Preface		9
CHAPTER I	My Pre-Tertiary Education	13
CHAPTER II	Orientation and First Phase at Fourah Bay College	26
CHAPTER III	My Return to the University	34
CHAPTER IV	Extermination Attempts	46
CHAPTER V	My First Year in Final Year	55
CHAPTER VI	The Revelation	63
CHAPTER VII	My Final Year in Final Year	72
CHAPTER VIII	The Graduation Ceremony	81
CHAPTER IX	Getting Through a University	88
CHAPTER X	The True Success Equation	102
CHAPTER XI	Chase It!	107
CHAPTER XII	Are You a Student?	115
Addendum		122

CHAPTER I

My Pre-Tertiary Education

Heaving through a third year in final year was a humiliating exercise. Fragmented thoughts of inexorable experiences continually overpowered my inner man, as my projected last year at the University multiplied by a factor of three.

'Engineering students, who are really strong in Mathematics, always do well in the Electrical department, but I don't know why you are having problems'. That was the reaction of my Power Engineering Lecturer, Mr. Kebbie, as I failed his final year module for the second time. Decoding the trouble of my double repetition appeared as another Design Project, in partial fulfilment of an Engineering Bachelor. The rails of my academic dream crippled, as I watched the reinforced foundation slowly settle, and all I could see was a brilliant delay. As I struggled, friends and family began to assault my genuinely-earned intellectual skills, especially in the precinct of Mathematics. Even to me, I started looking like a boob. I began to lose trust in my educational strength. And, covertly, I initiated a self-appraising algorithm to verify my true mental capacity. 'But how about my pre-Tertiary Education?' I pondered. 'How about my academic life prior to University?'

My gambolling and interacting with family members, at home, were minimized when parents realized my reasoning strength was due to actively engage in academic work. I bypassed the Kindergarten process and entered straight into the first class of Services Children's School, located close to the 34th military hospital, Wilberforce, Freetown, at a very tender age. The school was military-owned, under the leadership of Mrs. Ethel Mbayo. My teachers were very fond of me, for I was the youngest at that level – Class I. My acuity was demonstrated in a number of occasions, both in and out of the classroom. In my second class, I used to fluently read passages of my school reader. I participated in quiz competitions and other extracurricular activities, and playing soccer every evening became an addiction.

Just when school broke up one afternoon, in Class III, a strange man appeared, requesting to take me home in the guise of being sent by my elder brother, Ismaila. Dad used to send a military driver to pick us from school. On some occasions, he showed up himself. But when he had a busy schedule, Ismaila would pick me up, as a road-accident precautionary measure. That unknown man emphasized my brother was busy and would not be in a position to take me home on that day. It was a period in which kids were being kidnapped for demonic rituals! In my premature state, I was totally ignorant of his intention and almost yielded, as my bag had been handed to him already. That's what I usually did. Whenever they picked me up from school, I just handed my school bag over to whosoever received me. As I initiated the first few steps with him, something popped up on my mind and I responded 'But I don't know you and my brother could've informed me'. As he tried wheedling me, I spotted Ismaila from afar. Instantaneously, I shouted, 'look at my brother coming!' The guy dashed into a nearby corner with a very high velocity, jumped into a car and drove off; he had a parked car and there was another man in the vehicle, as well. This I explained to my brother, who strictly cautioned me not to give-in to any of those attempts, except from someone at home. We safely arrived home, but my bag was never retrieved.

When I got promoted to the sixth class, my father was posted to the second battalion of the Sierra Leone Army, Teko Barracks, in Makeni - a town located in the Northern Province of Sierra Leone. His posting created immense disorder in the family. My late father was a Muslim, an Alhaji, operating in Polygamy. At that time, he had four wives, with more than twenty children – more than ten girls and at least ten boys. He also looked after extended family members, some of whom were based at home. When he was transferred, he couldn't take everybody with him to Makeni, so he had to find an option. Some members were selected to travel with him, and others distributed to senior family members in Freetown. Some members rejected some, especially those who were in bad relationships. Some accepted some, but some relationships were a cat-and-mouse type. To preclude interruption of my schooling, I had to stay with an Aunt, one of my Mum's elder sisters, Aunt Mary Roberts, until the end of the academic year, when I joined other family members in Makeni.

In my new school, everybody, from fellow pupils to Headteacher, liked me so much and they all became my friends. My brilliance was also displayed at Services Primary School in academic work, and I also led devotional sessions a number of times, reading Biblical scriptures at every lead. It was another military-owned school, with similar nomenclature, where I stayed for an academic year.

My life in Makeni was difficult. Dad was a Major, but his appointment relied only on basic salary, which was not even enough to run the home, let alone for recreation.

It was like the whole barracks, and probably the town, was suffering from drought, as there was insufficient supply of water. We mired in hunger, relaxing in our beautiful military quarter. Famine was almost endemic because food supply was increasing inadequately. Makeni maintained a highly deplorable weather, which was torrid, with biting midges locally referred to as 'Moot-moot' – I believe more tormenting than mosquitoes. 'Moot-moot' made me inconvenient in Teko Barracks, one of the reasons I abhorred my stay in Makeni. Well, living conditions made some amount of progress when Dad was appointed Parliamentary Elections Officer. He was temporarily based in Magburaka, a few miles from Makeni town, where we used to go during weekends. In Magburaka, Dad had a conspicuous mango tree, in his quarter, from which he instructed maids to lop some fruits after ingesting opulent food. That tree was always healthy-looking, with matured fruits reserved for us. Varieties of food were always on Dad's table and we never thought of hunger. We hated moving back to Teko Barracks after weekend breaks, but the Elections period ended and Dad safely returned home.

Later, in Makeni, Dad proposed to another lady, Isatu, who started paying him visits, presenting delicious meals at every arrival. She appeared very nice to all at home and we did appreciate her. Not too long, that physically beautiful, tall, dark figure became Dad's fourth wife, because he got divorced from his third wife – Ngor Alice. So, my mother, Cecilia Nyangbe, became third and Isatu assumed fourth position.

My frustration enhanced when Dad received a heart-breaking message as he was putting on his usual smart military attire, at about 07:00 hours. A young man, believed to be a medical practitioner, walked into our residence, intimating Dad of my brother's moribund state. Sirmin, a six-month old baby who had already made walking attempts, was in intensive care at a hospital in Makeni, town, together with Mum. I could still figure him wrestling with me as we walked around the beautiful military officers' quarters in the cool of the day! That boy was 'beautiful', a true male version of my younger sister, Abibatu. Everybody in our neighbourhood liked him. Everywhere we went, people would admire him, and they always wanted to carry him. Probably, he could have started walking at about seven months old, which was the age I started walking. Or he could've even started earlier, because he was already making walking attempts and would leave a bed side-frame as he stood by it and smiled. In some instances, he would hold on to other stationary objects and walk by them. Major Koroma was an experienced father! When he got that breaking news, he couldn't continue dressing up, so other relations had to help him complete. He was a strong military man, and fought to maintain his composure. But how could you conceal an intense emotional torture? His eyes struggled to withhold a pool of water, fighting to separate itself from its source. From his face, you could sense a real battle between bravery and cowardice, which explained that psychosomatic torture can defeat even the strongest man in the universe. As a family, we immediately travelled to the hospital and as we approached the medical centre, we were faced with a devastating experience. Mum, a loving and caring mother, was genuinely weeping over her piddling gestation. Her visage totally transformed and it was easy to see that her emotions were horrendously battered. In agony, she was singing, in her Mende tribal language, 'be yae lima ay, ay nya lwi Sirmin be yae lima ay, lima ay, be yae lima...', meaning, 'where are you going, my child Sirmin...?' That was the first time I witnessed my mother tearing like an abandoned baby! Carrying a child for more than nine months in a natural incubator, and the only period you could physically spend with him was six months. How could she handle that? Members of the Koroma family couldn't stand it; we burst into tears as we consoled each other. I hated looking at corpses, but when Sirmin died, I held him in my arms as we bitterly wept while on our way home. As a little boy, I was afraid of seeing human remains, especially at night. But I held the late Sirmin wrapped in my arms, on my bed, right through the night, with tears all over, until it was time for burial the next day. Mum was emotionally wounded, working in trauma for months as she sang her consoling traditional song. The loss of Sirmin drilled a painful emotional gully in my heart. And for a while, I couldn't gain control of my schooling – I operated in absent-mindedness.

After Dad's second year in Makeni, he was posted back to Freetown and we happily travelled together. He took up another appointment, but this time it was an elevation. Dad became Camp Commandant of the Republic of Sierra Leone Army, based in Murray Town Barracks. Before and during his military career, he pursued National and International Accounting-related courses, which properly positioned him to become a very good Administrator. A few months later, I was at the Old Railway Line residence of one of my elder sisters, Sabiatu, on a particular date. Sabiatu is the recognized second daughter of Dad and the first daughter of Ngor Mamanyor – Dad's second wife. Sabi, or Hinga, as she's commonly known by family members and very close friends, was a very strong and committed member of the New Testament Bible Church in Sierra Leone. She sometimes took me to some of their services and I almost became a regular member of their Ministry. Even before I travelled to join Dad in Makeni, I was supposed to get an annual Award on Memory Verse Recital at their Collegiate Drive Congo Cross Sanctuary. I actually started learning the Truth about Jesus Christ at the New Testament Bible Church, then pastored by the Late Brother Bill Kallon and his wife Sister Doris Kallon. When we received the exhilarating news that Dad had been promoted to the rank of a substantive Lieutenant Colonel, and was allocated an official quarter at Wilberforce Barracks, Off Hill Station, adjacent to Peekay Lodge, together we jubilated, waiving the episode of misery. Life became better - an immense improvement. There were no more droughts, no more hunger, and no more 'Moot-moots'. We started leading the life of the children of a noble statesman. But Dad's elevated financial status attracted polygamist expansion. He married a fifth wife, Bintu, commonly called Glorjy, and his children increased to more than thirty – even though he lost some. Bintu was a frisky type who interacted with family members at all levels.

Prior to our return to Freetown, the designation of my former school in Freetown was modified from Services Children's School to Services Primary School. Before we departed Makeni, I got promoted to the seventh class, and so my return to Services Primary School in Freetown was a continuation. The new Head of the school was Mrs. Phelix George. Fellow pupils, teachers, Headteacher... they all missed me in Makeni, but my pilgrimage was unavoidable. In life, people lose people. But humanly, to every loss, there is a gain. Friends in Makeni mourned my departure, while those in Freetown celebrated my arrival. I lost friends in Makeni, but gained friends in Freetown.

On my first day, I joined the class with a test on dictation and spelling! In spite of the fact that I was new, I was fourth in the test, in a class of more than fifty. The teacher was very much delighted in my performance, and fellow classmates strengthened their relationships with me.

It was time for the Selective Entrance Examinations - the examinations we wrote before graduating from primary school. I got into the exam hall, at Collegiate Secondary School, in Freetown, at about 07:00 hours, while Ismaila waited outside the building. Some hours later, I finished and we were heading home. A few months later, the results were announced and I had a good grade, which was not a surprise to friends and family. The Prince of Wales School, the alma mater of Ismaila, was my first choice and I attained an aggregate above their threshold. Prince of Wales School was located in Kingtom, the central part of Freetown. On the day of the interview, I was late, and my name had been passed already. My father reported the case and I was recalled; successfully, I went through the second interview and commenced secondary school in 'One Crimson', which was the best class. We started classes, wrote the first test in Mathematics, and I obtained 100%. My then Mathematics teacher, who was a lady, the late Mrs. Sesay, liked me so much and encouraged me to keep up the good work.

The promotional examinations approached and we got into the hall for the written History assessment. Our teacher was Mr. Abass Collier and I was one of his best pupils in that subject. I was settled, well-prepared for that examination and believed nothing could stop me from making 100%, which I did earlier. At that level, History was mostly about dates and events, so it was easy to get 100%, if you understood well. The Question-and-Answer scripts were distributed; I read through and realized my 100% was sure. But as soon as I picked up my writing tool to start work, a very high fever overshadowed me. Why? I could not understand. I started shivering as my chair and table vibrated with me. In seconds, I regurgitated on my script, and couldn't write a single character. The invigilators tried to bring me round, but to no success. Immediately, I was conveyed home by my then Physical Education teacher, the late Mr. John M.S. Bull, and was subsequently taken to the hospital. I could not write that paper, but my teacher evaluated me based on records.

At the Prince of Wales School, I had a good time and was later joined by my brother, Jamiru. Jamiru was very clever. He was excellent, especially in Arts subjects, and was also admitted into 'One Crimson'. For the first three years, Jamiru was the best pupil, not only in his class, but the entire school as a whole at his level, as he passed with the highest percentages on average. During prize-giving ceremonies, he used to receive lots of prizes, which attracted huge attention to his outstanding performance. Dad, himself, used to drive us to and fro school, but when he had a busy schedule, he ordered one of his drivers to perform that onus. Moinya and Kadi, two of my elder sisters, were at the Methodist Girls' High School and Saint Joseph's Secondary School respectively. Moinya is a daughter of Ngor Mamanyor and Kadi is my mother's first-born. St. Joseph's Convent Secondary School is also the alma mater of Jorbay, who is the last-born of Grandma Nancy – Dad's first wife. Jorbay and Kadi were very close. She was a real mentor for Kadi, and taught her the youthful principles of life. A greater part of Kadi's exposure, especially during schooling, originated from Jorbay. Dad normally picked up me and Jamiru from school, then Kadi and Moinya, and we would all go to the supermarket, where he got us sweeties and other stuff before driving home. I could remember one of his Lebanese friends, Mr. Kay, who owned a supermarket where he used to take us. We loved Dad so much because he truly honoured his responsibilities as a father. Even in the midst of polygamy, he cared for us and did not discriminate amongst siblings of different maternal backgrounds. To me, his biological fatherhood is irreplaceable.

In my third form, we got ready for the promotional examinations and History again. History was my best Arts subject and I expected nothing less than 95%. One of my close friends, Anthony Sinnah, who lived in my neighbourhood, met me at home at approximately three hours before the test. That was our routine. We used to go together, especially during examinations period. Well, we had some time and had completed studying. So I chose a movie and we watched it in a chilled mood. Later, I glanced at the wall clock and realized it had passed the start time already. 'Shabad!' I shouted (as my friend was so nicknamed). I rushed outside and screamed one of our drivers' names. Together, we jumped into the vehicle and, as soon as we arrived into the examination hall, the Invigilator announced 'ten minutes more'. That was another History examination gone. Why? I couldn't figure it out. I almost wept, but maintained some amount of emotional strength. Tony and I requested question papers and answer scripts. The Invigilator denied us, but we pleaded, and he accepted our appeal. I tried to put down some information, but what do you expect in less than ten minutes for a three-hour paper? I did my best and handed over the paper. The Results were out and I made 48%.

At the Prince of Wales School, we didn't just walk into Streams. The School Authorities allocated us based on previous academic performance. I got promoted to the fourth form and was invited to the Science Stream. Dad was very happy because he had longed for one of his children to get into Sciences and become a medical doctor. From a close family source, two of my elder siblings, Lt. Col. (Rtd.) Andrew F. Koroma and Bialo, who happened to be the recognized first son and first daughter of Dad respectively, opted for Sciences but withdrew shortly. Not that they were stupid, but were not cut out for Sciences, as they excelled in Arts subjects. Andy, as we used to refer to Andrew, is the first-born of Grandma Nancy, whilst Bialo is the first daughter of Grandma Nancy. Bialo also used to take me to 'Jesus is Lord' Ministries at Wilberforce, pastored by Sister Dora Dumbuya. I also got some Teachings on Jesus Christ there, though on few occasions.

My first tuition in Form Four-Sciences was on Additional Mathematics; Binomial Theorem. Gosh, the teacher was so rough with the factorial notation ^nC_r... Imagine a pupil just from third form, not used to that stuff; he wasn't encouraging. Some of my classmates immediately left for the General-stream. The General-stream was an amalgam of both Arts and Science Courses. You didn't do much of Sciences, and had an option not to offer Additional Mathematics. In about two weeks, a few followed, but most of us decided to stay and face the challenge. At the end of that tuition, I was upset, a state that was no different from my friends'. It was time to go home; the driver arrived and I left disappointed. I couldn't explain anything to anybody, and just went to bed without food. The next evening, I approached a guy in my neighbourhood, Junior Adeola. This guy was an Electrical Engineering student at Fourah Bay College, and I revealed my problem with Binomial Theorem. He offered me an extra tuition, and I realized Binomial Theorem was nothing complex - just that our teacher was not careful. I got better in Additional Mathematics and when we wrote the first class-test, I obtained 73%, which was not the best, but one of the best grades. I started talking the language of Additional Mathematics.

In school, I was not all about Sciences. I was not all academic, but very much interested in Soccer, which I always played - it was my hobby. I played it both at home and school, but this didn't affect my academic performance negatively. It was an exercise. At about age fifteen, I became a member of my school Soccer and Volleyball teams. At my first Volleyball attempt, we played up to the Semi-finals, which according to our then Physical Education teacher, was the first time for that school to get to that level and I was the best Server of my team – I made so many points during serving. But we lost to Ahmadiyya Muslim Secondary School. They were our 'big brothers'. Most of us were tiny teenagers, ranging from fifteen to eighteen, whilst they were mostly muscular adults. We couldn't stand them. I didn't play Soccer that year because it clashed with the Inter-Secondary School Volleyball Competition. Soccer was actually my first choice, but two of my close friends were eliminated from the Soccer team during trials. I was bored and decided to stay with them in the Volleyball team. My coach, the Physical Education teacher, Mr. J.M.S. Bull, tried all he could to keep me in the Soccer team, because I was the best player for the number-nine wing. But he couldn't. He had also seen Ismaila play, in the School team, in his days and did very well. Ismaila also played in the number-nine wing. Ismaila played up to first-division Soccer in Sierra Leone – for the Freetown United Soccer Club, and then relocated to London after about six months, but didn't pursue his Soccer dream. So Mr. J.M.S. Bull knew we had the talent. However, I wasn't happy because the Soccer team didn't do well that year – they were eliminated in an early stage.

When I was about to write my Ordinary Level Examinations, my father retired from the Army, during the National Provisional Ruling Council (NPRC) Regime, then headed by Captain Valentine Strasser who was later replaced by Brigadier General Julius Maada Bio. His retirement was abnormal, followed by an abrupt difficulty. For weeks, he couldn't communicate with us. He was just going out in the morning and coming in very late at night. Why? I couldn't perceive. I had no idea of what was going on, and nor did anyone else, except his wives and some of my elder siblings. This forced me to stop schooling as the situation exacerbated. I had started having extra English Language classes with Madam Johnson-Cole, but discontinued as well. Madam Johnson-Cole was a teacher of the Methodist Girls' High School and one of the Examiners of the West African Examinations Council, renowned for her academic excellence, especially in English Language. She's actually one of the Mentors who began activating my writing skill. I could remember the first passage she gave me to summarize on my first extra class with her. In the passage, some events happened and the questions that followed asked to state the events that transpired. The first event was the fall of the Roman Empire. So, the first statement I listed was 'The Fall of the Roman Empire'. I thought my English Language was excellent, but she said 'No, Samuel, it should be 'The Roman Empire Fell' because you're reporting – it must be in the past'. Since then, my eyes began to open in the area of English Language. That's how a lot of students failed. Sometimes, students failed, not that they didn't have the talent, not because they were stupid, not because they were lazy, not because they were misplaced, but because they had no good Mentor. Later, I registered for the Ordinary Level Examinations just to earn myself a Secondary School graduating Certificate. Actually, I didn't prepare well for it, but attained a third division with some credits. I couldn't continue schooling because I didn't even obtain a University requirement. My elder brother, Lt. Col. (Rtd.) Andrew Foday Koroma, was then Commanding Officer of the Fourth Battalion of the Sierra Leone Army, who promised to let me join my elder siblings in London, and continue my education. During that period, clubbing, partying, going to the gym, Basketball, Soccer, Table Tennis, and other recreational activities were all I was engaged in, hoping to travel. Up to the point of this account, I couldn't explain the reason for that breach.

About two years later, some of my former classmates, which included Issa Toure and Anthony Sinnah, and my immediate elder sister Kadi, advised me to get back to school and continue my coursework. They knew I was brilliant, but was somehow distracted by that London promise. That was a very difficult decision to make. I was shy as most of my contemporaries had gone ahead. I didn't want to become their subordinate in academic pursuit. But swallowed my pride, informed my parents who sponsored me and I started having private classes. I didn't enrol at my alma mater, Prince of Wales School, but registered privately. During classes, I was renowned for academic excellence and was the best pupil among those present. There were Advanced Level students as well, who wanted to improve on their past grades, but none of them could match up to my touchstone. My General Mathematics and Additional Mathematics teacher, Mr. Kamara, who was a teacher of the Government Rokel Secondary School, liked me so much and informed other pupils that up to that time, I was the best pupil he ever taught. Two of my mates, at private classes, were Samuel Bondi and Fatmata Kargbo. Samuel Bondi was very good in Chemistry; in fact he was the best in Chemistry, in that class. We wrote the Ordinary Level Examinations and I emerged with fascinating grades, with a distinction in General Mathematics among other very good grades, as expected by my teacher and classmates.

Succeeding the release of our results, I gained admission into The Sierra Leone Grammar School to pursue my Advanced Level Course; I registered for Mathematics, Physics, Chemistry and General Paper. Reader, there's immense difference between Fifth-form and Sixth-form, but with perseverance and hard work, I was somehow comfortable. The Additional Mathematics background earned me a very good foundation for the Advanced Level Course. My best subject at A-Levels was Applied Mathematics, taught by Mr. George Kobba. For you to excel in Applied Mathematics, you have to be well grounded in the principles of Physics and Pure Mathematics.

My life at The Sierra Leone Grammar School was somehow boring. Yes, I was satisfied with the coursework, and was also a member of the Diogramix social club - a blend of pupils of The Sierra Leone Grammar School, mostly sixth-formers, and The Annie-Walsh Memorial School, in our days. We had lots of fun, but one thing I wasn't happy about was our non-involvement in Soccer. I really liked Soccer and wanted to put up my best performance at Sixth-form level. Some of my classmates, especially those from Prince of Wales School, were also good at playing Soccer, and we could have had a wonderful team. But our then Principal, Mr. Akiwande Josiah Lasite, did not permit us to participate in the Inter-Secondary School Soccer Competition. According to him, he wanted to preclude distraction and enable us concentrate on our coursework. To some extent, I enjoyed Athletics since I played casual Basketball, and did the Triple-jump during our Inter-house Athletics Sports Meet, at the National Stadium.

We took the examinations and I got promoted to Upper-sixth form. Initially, Applied Mathematics was a challenge to A-Level pupils. When Mr. Kobba started his tuition at Lower-sixth level, most of my classmates started having extra classes with him. Whether it was arranged by the teacher or fellow pupils, I couldn't tell. But I did not join them. Yes, when we started working on Applied Mathematics, it appeared difficult, but I like facing challenges, and so I decided to face the fight alone. I would be working in my bedroom, locked up. And when we had taken the first test in Applied Mathematics, Mr. Kobba uttered 'Congratulations, well done' as he handed me my marked test paper. He knew I wasn't part of his extra classes, but did very well. He spotted my Mathematical potential and later approached me one-on-one. He revealed that I was a potential 'A-student' in Mathematics and advised I join his extra classes, as he wanted to properly prepare me for the Advanced Level Examination to get nothing less than an 'A'. We started and he was coaching me on a one-on-one basis. As we got deeper into preparing for the A-Level Examinations, The Armed Forces Revolutionary Council, A.F.R.C., seized power from the first democratically-elected government of the late His Excellency Dr. Ahmad Tejan-Kabba on 25th May, 1997, which interrupted my schooling. Life in Sierra Leone, especially in Freetown, was unpredictable because the Regime of Major Johnny Paul Koroma was internationally unrecognized. Everything was like on a standstill. Workers were on a sit-down strike, food supply was short, prices escalated, electricity supply was inadequate and the country seemed ungovernable. But the atmosphere later pacified and we returned to school. In early 1998, about January, there was an invasion led by the ECOWAS Military Wing, ECOMOG, to topple Johnny Paul Koroma. ECOMOG and the A.F.R.C. were engaged in a fierce battle. We were locked up indoors for about a week, and after a day ceasing, some Indigenes migrated while others went in search of food. We moved to the western outskirts of the capital. That attempt by ECOMOG to topple the AFRC was unsuccessful. But a little over nine months of A.F.R.C.-rule, there was another attack. Johnny Paul Koroma fled. He was deposed and the democratic government of late President Tejan Kabba was restored. Even with the re-instatement of President Kabba, our security was not guaranteed.

On 6th January, 1999, there was an unsuccessful attempt by joint forces of the Revolutionary United Front and the Armed Forces Revolutionary Council, to topple President Tejan Kabba. Freetown was almost painted red with human blood, with the streets becoming a representation of a mortuary. Corpses could be seen in different locations on the streets, and whether the Indigenes would see the next sunrise always remained a mystery.

In March 1999, Kadi, who was then based in the United States, sponsored my air trip to Ghana. I travelled together with a younger cousin of mine, Ginah. According to our itinerary, we were supposed to transit in Abidjan, the Capital of the Ivory Coast, for a few hours, get other tickets and board a Ghana Airways Flight to Accra, the Capital of Ghana. But our flight was delayed in Freetown and, as we landed at the Houphouet Boigny Airport, we could see an opposing Aircraft on the Runway, tagged Ghana Airways, with our expected flight number on the side. We were total strangers in the Ivory Coast, and worse, it was a French-speaking country. How could we communicate? However, I spoke with a Sierra Leonean Lady, who was close to me on board, and she offered us accommodation at a comfortable residence – Villa 71. We stayed in Abidjan for a few days, and then left for Accra on board Ghana Airways. Ginah and I arrived at the Kotoka International Airport, and were warmly received by Moinya, my nephews John Kall Vandi and Jone Vandi, and my niece Jenneh Vandi – now Mrs. Nyorbay. In the morning, I located the West African Examinations Council and had a chat with one of the officials, who intimated to me that registration was closed, but promised to help me out. We made an appointment for a later date, on that day, I couldn't locate him. I couldn't register for the Advanced Level Examinations, which was the primary requirement for the College of Medicine and Allied Health Sciences. I enquired at Legon University if I could be admitted for Medicine with my Ordinary Level Results, but they insisted on Advanced Level Grades or West African Senior School Certificate Examinations - WASSCE Qualifications. Also, I travelled to Kumasi, the Asante Region where the Kwame Nkrumah University of Science and Technology was located, to see if I could gain entrance to study Engineering. They also requested A-Levels or a WASSCE Certificate. Again, I made

Inquiries at the Ghana International School to enable me write the London A-Level Examinations, but all efforts required me to await another academic year.

During my wait, John Vandi took me around town and helped to familiarize me with some areas, especially Labadi Beach, where the famous Five-star Lapalm Royal Beach Hotel was planted. I also played Table Tennis a number of times at a Sports Club, located in North Kaneshie.

One evening, Moinya asked me to accompany her to visit a friend who lived at a hostel in our neighbourhood. We arrived at Akrowa House at about 18:00 hours and stepped into the compound, in which there were groups of grown boys and girls - the bulk of which were students of the London School of Graduates. It was an Institution that offered Courses for the award of British qualifications. On entry into the compound, there were a set of girls on an African couch, one of whom was my sister's friend, who offered us comfortable sitting positions. Moinya introduced me and we all exchanged greetings. Just when we entered the compound, I glanced at a dark, slim girl, with bulky eyes like those of Kadi. As I sat in their midst, she was totally focused on me, and reciprocating views became a practice of that period. We were both attracted to each other, but I thought it was infatuation. Many times, love at first sight is considered fragile, but sometimes deep intimacy, enough to distort existing marital bonds, emanates from hidden traits of infatuation. I was jittery, and secretly informed my sister, 'it's time for home'. We left and that same evening, I met with a boy, Alexander Afenyo, who was one of the students of London School of Graduates. He was very nice to me and we became friends.

Our friendship continued, and the keeper of my secret affinity was unfolded - Clarissa Esi Acquaah. Alex revealed everything about her, and the more we discussed, the more I increased in passion, because she was the exact kind of personality I desired. Later, Alex informed me Clarissa was also investigating me, which inspired me to book an appointment. I arrived. Clarissa looked right into my eyes and I reciprocated. Her straight nose and captivating eyes set the stage of burning desire for an opposing gender. The radiation from her smiles transmitted ripples just sufficient to support an established blind date. And it was like our emotions were triggered by the same pulse of a monostable timing circuit. I couldn't control my breathing. I tried to utter a word, but couldn't. Without saying a letter, she knew all on my mind. She knew I was into her, but needed a verbal expression from her prospective partner. Suddenly, I just said, 'Clarissa, I love you'.

'I love you too', she replied. My relief valve opened! And I was back to my normal blissful state. At that point, I was in great joy as if my name had been written in the

Book of Life. That was the start of a new episode in my love life. Clarissa was exceptional. She was intelligent, serious, beautiful, trustworthy, hard-working, and above all, God-fearing. She was just complete. Except for her schooling, we were at most times together. And dining with her never made me want to give up using the cutlery, as she scooped clustered particles of sumptuous victuals. Her strong Protestant belief was demonstrated as she walked me in and out of a prayer house on Sundays. During that period, we attended Trade Fairs and hooked up at Boom Erang Night Club. We also visited the Accra Mall and many other recreational centres.

Later, Kadi and I started making arrangements for me to join her in the United States, but nothing worked and she advised me to get back home and pursue a University Bachelor Course. I posed a question to Clarissa saying, 'Clarissa, my sister wants me to get back home and continue schooling, to pursue a Bachelor Course, what do you think?' 'Samou', she replied, 'if you can gain admission into a University here, fine. But, if you can't, wherever you're admitted, go. I love you, I'd be missing you, but it's in the interest of progress'. She continued, 'Please stay in touch, okay? Don't stop communicating okay?' That's the voice of someone without a selfish vision. She loved me; she'd be missing me, but was ready to give me up for a period, in the interest of academic success. We were both moved with compassion, but got settled on the matter.

I got attired on the day of my departure to Sierra Leone, accompanied by Clarissa, Moinya, John, Jone, and Jenneh, and headed to the Kotoka International Airport. Clarissa was moved with sentiment. She couldn't look me in the eye, but our temporary separation was inevitable. I had to leave. I had to be a man. It was a must. We took lots of photographs, and I boarded the flight some minutes after checking in. Approximately three hours later, I disembarked at the Lungi International Airport, now Freetown International Airport, and sailed home safely via a dilapidated ferry. On arrival, I was informed of a girl who made frequent calls, trying to verify my safe arrival. A few minutes later, the phone rang. I picked up, and a familiar female voice, which sometimes appeared to repair my eardrums from infected statements, emanated. I wasn't surprised. That was my expectation. I wasn't on a cell phone, so I gave her my landline number. 'Oh, Samou! I've been trying to verify your safe arrival', Clarissa reacted. 'Are you okay?' That's the voice of someone with a sense of responsibility. We chatted for some time until she turned off the communication signal. Esi and I constantly communicated on the Internet, through e-mails, and gave me repeated landline calls. We were apart, but continually talking to each other made our relationship stronger as though we were glued together.

■■■

CHAPTER II

Orientation and First Phase at Fourah Bay College

Fourah Bay College, University of Sierra Leone, was the key institution of learning in West Africa; hence, Sierra Leone earned the name 'The Athens of West Africa'. Initially, it was established to transmit the gospel of Jesus Christ, but later transformed into offering courses in various fields. Students from different parts of West Africa, like Nigeria, Ghana and the Ivory Coast, attended that noble institution.

Fourah Bay College later merged with Njala University to form the central University of Sierra Leone. After a while, Fourah Bay College and Njala separated, and now The University of Sierra Leone is made up of Fourah Bay College, College of Medicine and Allied Health Sciences, Institute of Public Administration and Management, and the School for Postgraduate Studies. Currently, Fourah Bay College is located at Mount Aureol, around the outskirts of Freetown, and offers courses in Engineering, Arts, Law, and many other fields. The undulating hill, as you descend from campus, puts you in readiness of an emerging danger.

I travelled to Freetown, the capital of Sierra Leone, in August 1999 to complete my University Admissions Process. Prior to arriving in Freetown, my elder brother, Freeman, submitted an application form for Engineering on my behalf, as instructed by my parents, and I was invited to interview. I had the academic pre-requisites to study for a Bachelor's in Engineering, in Sierra Leone, but to verify my competence, as other institutions did I needed to go through the process of Interview. Successfully, I went through the interview, headed by the then Deputy Registrar Mr. S.N. Dumbuya. I was admitted into the Faculty of Engineering and advised to get ready for orientation, and hence for University work, in October.

Students from different backgrounds hurried into Fourah Bay College campus as they zealously fought to fulfil their academic destinies. Prior to proper practical engagement with College curriculum, the three-day exciting orientation programme was sufficient to get students ready for the actual academic chase. The seminars started in the morning, at about 08:00 hours, after breakfast. The first session continued until it was time for a one-hour lunch break at approximately 12:00 hours. Teachings were received from those with different personalities, mostly lecturers who dealt with us directly in our various faculties. We were taught on the University Setting and slowly delved into the Fourah Bay College affair. New entrants were informed about the different faculties and their locations, various disciplines offered and other opportunities related to student benefits. During and after tuition, a period of interaction in the form of question-and-answer sessions followed. I could remember when a colleague, Desmond Benya, asked a question that sent the whole class laughing. He said, 'If I should loquaciously philosophize...' Freshmen did not even await his ending, and the class was hilariously toppled. The tutor at that time was Mrs. Emmerson-Thomas, who also laughed, but intimated to us that it was a very good approach. She emphasized that as University students, when we speak, people should deduce our educational level. Desmond was serious about his question, but a major goal of it was to overturn the classroom into a laughing cafeteria, which he achieved. He was comic and no doubt he partially pursued a 'jester' career on his public speaking platform. On the completion of lectures, freshmen rushed into their dormitories, at about 18:00 hours, after having a meal prepared by university authorities.

The orientation programme was not only limited to events of the Fourah Bay College prospectus. Dating events, some of which led to successful marriages, transpired. There was an inter-sex relationship ban, and cross-hostel activities were forbidden by orientation regulations. But how could you sever the mating of desperate grown-ups? During nights, you could see opposing sexes moving around like registered continuing students – utilizing their three-day residential status. They seemed very much familiar with campus routes, and detecting their status as freshmen was almost impossible. Social clubs on campus also began their campaign processes – in attempts to depopulate rival associations. However, I successfully went through the orientation and started lectures in October.

I was admitted into the preliminary year and resided on campus with a colleague, Bainda, of a different faculty. He was in the faculty of Social Sciences and Law, but we had a good time though there were some disparities. We were both studious, but I was interested in social and some extra-curricular activities, as opposed to his inclination. I had intimate girlfriends, and whenever they paid me visits, I had to kick him out of the room - I factorized him, as we used to say. We quarrelled at a time when one of my girlfriends, Tutu, stepped into our room. My roomie was reluctant to move out - he tried to be defiant, but we later resolved the issue and I had good time with my then girlfriend. Tutu was like another form of Clarissa, except that she was bigger in size. We were not only in a relationship, but lived like true siblings. We were not living in the same home, but distinguishing between hers and mine could only be verified by close friends and relations.

Politically, Fourah Bay College was divided into two camps: the White and Black camps. I belonged to the White camp, usually referred to as the 'Generals'. 'Generals' was made up of a political club, Liberals, and other social clubs. The parent club of the social clubs, of the White camp, was the Quimanora club. The Quimanora, abbreviated 'Q', was the most outstanding club, not only on Fourah Bay college campus, but the entire University of Sierra Leone and the student-body country-wide. Quimanora controlled lots of other junior clubs, some of which included Cyclades, Paciphix, Embala, Strovecs and Madrugar. There were also Fraternities like Concordia, Areopagus and Excelsior, which portrayed neutral images on campus, but were hidden supporters of camps. There were also Sororities like Azalea, as well. Some clubs were typically composed of boys, some girls and others a blend. The female wing of Quimanora was referred to as the Deflosacs, abbreviated Deflo. The Black camp was made up of a parent-political-club 'Auradicals' and other social clubs like Klymax, Syramax, Dahlia and Magma.

In my preliminary year, both camps invited me to be part of their organizations. For a while, I was undecided, but later made up my mind to get into the White camp, as I loved their system of operation. I got initiated into the Cyclades club under the Leadership of Seray, and the Concordia fraternity - the Grand Master of which was Sidris. Cyclades club was very interactive and most of her activities were concerned with organizing parties and outings. We also organized inter-club soccer matches, the interaction of which facilitated friendship among students, even of different universities and colleges.

The initiation process of Cyclades was in the form of an outing and bottle party. It was very much open! There was nothing hidden. Invitations were dispensed to other students and people outside the club, and the university as well. As the process began, initiates queued around the beach, as they sang songs taught by members of the club. Sometimes we 'bubu-danced' - a traditional musical group using bamboos as trumpets, beating drums and playing other native instruments alongside songs. During that period, we sometimes received minor torture in the form of slaps and nips, discharged by members. Later, we did some jogging and other physical exercises on the seaside which sailed us to the final stage. As we lay fatigued, resulting from the physical exercises, every initiate was prostrate on the seashore, with only shorts on, as members began the scrubbing process. With our backs faced up, members scooped some sand which was used to carry out the scrubbing event on our backs. That painful activity continued until our backs oozed out fluid or even blood. Imagine the point at which salty sand is being rubbed against a tender skin. Sometimes, we screamed without rescue. Finally, senior members threw you into the sea, as a symbol of completion. But when that wounded skin and the salty solution intersected, it was as if spicy fluid had been poured into your naked eyes. However, the initiation wrapped up with the bottle beach party, during which we interacted with our girlfriends, senior members, past members and other invited guests, especially fellow students. The beach party helped us to not even realize the intensity of the pain.

The Concordia fraternity was more engaged in formal and semi-formal activities. We organized dinners, cocktails and, unavoidably, initiation processes. We were also trained to excel in academia. I remember when I was late for a session and asked to write an article on the topic 'Ghost', after receiving some lashes that got me crying. Impromptu speeches were also provoked by members of the cult. As an initiate, you were taught lots of ethical principles, some of which helped put you on good footing to face the secular and sacred world. Elders mentored us on the use of cutlery, how to handle your wife or fiancée when you go on a date, and positive moral values were imparted into us. Furthermore, we were challenged with Biblical scriptures which they instructed us to recite, like Psalms 1. In some cases, we carried out fake activities like invoking dead spirits. Sometimes, initiates were locked up in coffins, and other times, members chased you in unknown destinations with your eyes truly tied, and so you didn't recognize anything happening around you. Most of these activities were executed in the dark, around campus. One practice I never got an answer for was why we always entered fraternity sessions walking backwards.

Clubbing downtown was another hobby, but that never negatively affected my academic performance, as I always prioritized my activities and made proper schedules. For instance, if I had to attend a party on Saturday night, I read during the day to compensate for that future loss. On campus, I attended most of the major social club functions, which included parties, dinners and cocktails together with my then closest male friend Bolaji. He was in another faculty. Bolaji was also very close to Alfred, who was in the Faculty of Social Sciences and Law, and a member of the Quimanora Club. So we all attended most of the Campus social functions together. I later had a close female friend on campus called Lambri. Lambri and I were almost too-close friends and met at most of the social club functions, but I never knew how to define that relationship.

It was time for the preliminary year examinations, as we wrote one end-of-year examination. The courses we offered included Mathematics, Physics, Chemistry, Descriptive Engineering, Engineering Drawing I and Foundation Course. Some students who knew me only on campus were uttering all sorts of pessimistic statements about my future academic performance. But those who knew me in school before university did not. I was actively involved in social activities, so they thought I was going to mess up. When you failed in the preliminary year, you get expelled. That was their expectation: my expulsion. Naturally, I don't study a lot to understand, except if there was need. Academically, I learn easily - that's how God wired me. Humanly, I had the power to pass and I had the power to fail. In spite of my social involvement, my reasoning power was demonstrated in two of the class tests we wrote before the examinations, one in Chemistry and the other in Engineering Drawing I. In Chemistry, the lecturer wrote his questions on the board - there were four. I was about to begin the third question when I noticed an error. It was on Thermochemistry! The lecturer wrote a wrong ionic equation. That was an error you only recognize when you're truly grounded in that course. I brought it to the attention of the lecturer, who only accepted it after I gave him a valid chemical explanation; he then replaced the ionization reaction with the true atomization reaction. We completed the test, and I obtained a good grade. We took the preliminary year examinations, in which I did well, but was referred in Engineering Drawing I, meaning that I was to take a reference examination in it. Probably I truly failed that course, but let me notify you of an incident.

When we wrote our first class test in Engineering Drawing I, to my knowledge, I was second; I obtained 3.75/5, which was 75%. The first student was a boy from Murialdo Secondary School, Momoh. He got 4.5/5, which was 90%. We were not surprised, because Murialdo School offered Engineering Drawing as part of their curriculum; I only started doing Engineering Drawing at the University. But I respected Momoh so much because he was not the only student from that school; he was also outstanding in Drawing – especially Machine Drawing. A lot of students obtained low grades, which drove our lecturer to resolve that students should start attending extra classes organized by him. I replied, 'Sir, I don't have a problem with drawings. So for me, there's no need'. That's how we ended that episode; I did not attend the extra classes. In preparation for the reference examination, the lecturer again organized another extra class. I was swimming in a pool of perplexity. I trusted in my mental strength. I believed in my Drawing skill, but in our institutions, lecturers had the ability to fail who they wanted to, and pass who they wanted to pass. At that time, when a student failed a subject, he would be expelled. I was afraid because I didn't want to be debarred, so I joined the other students who couldn't pass that course. But listen to this! Our Drawing Lecturer, Mr. Moore, was not the tutor of his extra classes. There was another man who stepped into his shoes: one of his juniors at the Milton Margai College of Education and Technology. Mr. Moore was also working with The Milton Margai College of Education and Technology. He was head of the Mechanical Engineering department.

But his junior guy was good. Initially, he posted Drawing problems on the board to identify our strengths and weaknesses, earning him a clue of where to begin. He gave us questions on Isometric, Oblique and Orthographic views - which included first and third angle projections. Every time he moved around, he would find me doing the right thing. And at a point, that dude couldn't hold it and commented, in his exact words, 'I don't know why you were referred?' I asked why, and he continued, 'because you are producing expected results of all problems'. I just smiled and replied, 'I don't know either'. The guy remarked, 'you just go home and draw', and that was the end of my extra tuition. We took the examination. I got a 'B' and was promoted to the intermediate year of the Engineering course.

Normally, freshmen and continuing students played a Soccer match during the academic year. As a freshman, the continuing students' team was short of players, and I was invited by one of the continuing students, Aiah Kortequee, to join them, which I did. We had an exciting match in which continuing students won by a single goal scored by me. According to some colleagues, that was the first time continuing students defeated freshmen, or probably after a very long period. In reality, they did not win, because I was a freshman. The Engineering society, our Engineering organization on campus, hosted an end-of-year party at the end of every academic year. We partied, danced and had lots of fun.

Lectures started for the intermediate year and the usual hard work began. My study-mate was Ishmael Lisk. Ishmael was very studious! In most occasions, we practised electrical modules together. I still remember when we were working on some digital electronics problems on Boolean algebra. He was brilliant, but had great respect for me during our study. Ishmael was very hardworking and there was a feature about him I admired the most. When he was taught on a particular subject, he never went to bed until he comprehended everything. Sometimes, he would chase senior students of our faculty when he needed additional tuition. Ishmael and I were a good study team and I couldn't remember the two of us giving up on a problem. We always had a fruitful solution. But the problem was that I was not always around, as I was into social club activities, so our team was sometimes handicapped. 'Ish', as he was commonly called, was a member of one of the fraternities on campus. But fraternities didn't take up much time and they highly respected academic involvements.

Our Engineering society was a member of the International Association for the Exchange of Students for Technical Experience - IAESTE. Applications were usually invited from senior students - qualifying year to final year - to participate in International student exchange programmes. In that programme, students were exchanged amongst different countries who were members of IAESTE. Some pursued short courses, while others gained technical experience in other areas. I was a junior student, but forwarded an application! According to the lecturer who was in charge that was the first time an intermediate-year student applied for the IAESTE Scholarship. It was time for the interview and we were invited. The interview was dominated by final-year students, with me as the only intermediate-year student. That interview was very technical, and I will quote what the chairman of the panel, Dr. Bah, said as I correctly answered the first few questions: 'Samuel, if you're given the chance, you would contest for the Engineering presidency'. I smiled without uttering a word. Only senior students were permitted to contest for the Engineering society leadership, so he emphasized that point because I was very much vivacious at the interview. The shortlist was posted and I was among the only nine students selected for the exchange programme; mine was to Ghana at The Cocoa Research Institute. It was a partial scholarship, because you bought your ticket and they provided you accommodation. Kadi, again, bought my air ticket and I started making travelling arrangements. I was supposed to receive my documents from Ghana before departing, but my Faculty advised me to travel and contact the IAESTE Office at the University of Science and Technology in Ghana. Probably those documents are still in the post as I write. However, Moinya was still based in Accra, and I decided to make the trip and go to IAESTE Ghana in person.

I was in possession of my approving documents from my faculty. Clarissa was continually in touch with me and she knew everything. That time, I had a late flight and arrived at about 01:00 hours. Clarissa wanted to pick me up at the Airport, but I advised her to wait for security reasons. I went straight home to my sister, as I was no more a stranger. I was warmly received by Moinya and in the morning, about 07:00 hours, there was a knock on the front door. Moinya opened the door and someone stepped in: Clarissa. 'How did you know Samou was in here?' Moinya asked.' 'He called me', Clarissa replied. Clarissa and I had a lengthy chat and I later paid a visit to IAESTE at the Kwame Nkrumah University of Science and Technology, based in Kumasi, for verification. To my greatest surprise, they were totally ignorant of my exchange programme. Why? I couldn't comprehend. I tried locating the Cocoa Research Institute, but to no avail. I didn't even bother to inform my department back home because they couldn't contact IAESTE-Ghana whilst I was in Freetown, when my documentation was delayed - they only depended on hard copy mails. Then, I decided to spend my three-month vacation in Ghana, because Moinya was there and I was safe. I also needed some time with Clarissa.

During that vacation, a guy approached Moinya, requesting that I help some WASSCE, and prospective first-year university students, with Mathematics. My sister intimated to him earlier about my strength in Mathematics, and that I was an Engineering student of Fourah Bay College. The guy was Sierra Leonean, reading for a Master's Degree in Mining Engineering - in Ghana. He was Solomon Tucker. But I think he was so tied-up with his post-graduate course that he couldn't work with the students. So I was helping them in Further/Pure Mathematics, which helped me maintain the basics. If my Mathematics wasn't strong, I would have been embarrassed. But I successfully helped them and they were really impressed. Later, Kadi also tried to help me join her in the United States, considering the under-development of our country, including the low standards of education. We were at the verge of succeeding, so even when the vacation ended, I stayed there. But unfortunately, again, we lost the battle and I had to return home.

■■■

CHAPTER III

My Return to the University

I landed at the Lungi International Airport, now Freetown International Airport, on 14th November, 2001. The following day, I headed to the Faculty of Engineering to inform the Dean of my return and desire to continue my course. The Dean, then Dr. Redwood-Sawyerr, welcomed my idea, but I was referred to the College Registry, to pick up an academic course form. He underlined that all the forms in his possession had been utilized by other students. I wasted no time, went straight to the College Registry, and was sent back to the Dean for an approving document. The Dean of the faculty asked me to write a letter, requesting reinstatement. What? How could I apply for reinstatement when I completed the previous academic year? The academic year started in October and I arrived in November; why reinstatement? I was in a daze, but acted as instructed. I copied the Dean, the Deputy Registrar, and the then-principal of Fourah Bay College, Professor Strasser-King, who was a parent of my friend Michael Lawson. The process for my reinstatement was delayed until it was time for the first semester examinations. I was not permitted to take them, as I was not a registered student.

Most of my 'classmates' were already in the qualifying-year. Ishmael, my 'study mate', opted for the Electrical Engineering discipline. I had another 'classmate' in my neighbourhood, Khai Kallon. She was in the faculty of Pure and Applied sciences, with the Engineering option, so we offered some courses in common. When I enquired about Ishmael, Khai spoke very highly of him, and even revealed Ishmael was very good in electricals. In fact, according to Khai, Ishmael was top of the class. She says Professor Redwood-Sawyerr, who was also a final-year Lecturer in the Electrical department, always commented on Ishmael's performance as excellent. Professor Redwood-Sawyerr was the Lecturer for Signal Analysis, which most students considered the most difficult module in the electrical department. Ishmael's outstanding output was confirmed by my other 'contemporaries', who were together with him in the electrical department. I was so proud of him. Actually, I wasn't surprised, because he was intelligent and zealous. He was really dedicated to his coursework. However, I had to wait until the next academic year to continue my studies.

During my wait, the Cyclades club organized the normal initiation outing. It was in December. That year, it was hosted at the Goderich Police beach, very close to the Milton Margai College of Education and Technology campus. At Fourah Bay College, and probably other institutions, a member of a social club was always considered a member. When you completed your course, you were referred to as a 'past-member', with more dignity. I arrived in the afternoon, at the beach, and as soon as I entered, all my friends and other club members applauded my presence. They had missed me. This was a very interesting, and flamboyant, activity as lots of students and people from different Universities and work places patronized, irrespective of camp.

I changed into a beach costume and walked very close to the seashore for proper involvement in the initiation process. Suddenly, I turned against the sea, raised my head and a coincident vision of opposing sexes transpired - my eyes versus a female's. That girl was strange, and I believe I was also exotic in her sight. We were staring at each other from a distance of no less than hundred metres, as she was seated on the sand right at the top of the beach, where we usually kept our clothing and other material items. I got back into the initiation process to preclude suspicion. As I continued, rattling through me were thoughts of emotional occurrences, and every time I looked in her direction, our visions coincided. She was about 5ft. 9 in. tall. I believe we were attracted to each other. There were lots of girls around, but to me, she was outstanding. I couldn't concentrate on the initiation process and later approached one of my friends, D'Mills. On my return to the University, D'Mills was actually my closest male friend – so we discussed deep issues. From him, I enquired about that girl and her brief profile was revealed in a minute. She was a freshman of another club in the Black camp. I didn't meet her in person to avoid attracting attention of others. At that time, the camp distinction was not that prominent as we interacted at the highest level. I got her cell phone number from my friend and gave her a call the next day. She was very nice on the phone, in spite of the fact that she was talking to a stranger. She sounded decent. Briefly, I introduced myself, and she did the same. I tried to verify her description 'from the horse's mouth' to ensure I wasn't communicating with the wrong person. I was safe! We chatted for about two weeks, on the phone, and started getting interested in each other. It was like a blind date! To put an end to our imaginary conversation, we booked an appointment for an eye-to-eye consultation.

It was after the Christmas holidays and she was on the way to Fourah Bay College campus when her phone rang. She picked up and it was 'Samou'. That girl sounded very much exhilarated, and we agreed on meeting at Model Junction - the point around the central part of Freetown where we used to take cabs to and from Fourah Bay College Campus. She was very much intellectually-minded, though, and I didn't want to interrupt her academic schedule. I arrived at Model Junction, in the afternoon, and after a short while, a tall, dark, average-weighted, pink-lipped, bulky-eyed figure stepped out of a green and white mini-bus marked 'Fourah Bay College', from the college campus. Her peculiar hair styles and smart walk always reminded me of a typical young African Lady. She walked down, raised her head, and this 'extra beauty' headed towards me. This was not a mistake. She was the real personality. Something kept me bewildered for a while; there were other boys at the junction, but she just walked straight to me, without any form of signal, and I didn't even give her a description of my attire or position. I believe something orchestrated happened at the outing. Anyways, she walked towards me and said 'Samou?' I replied 'Amie'? We both nodded in agreement and I was led into a simple pub, just around Model Junction. As we sat, the first question I posed was 'Is this the person you were expecting? She replied 'yes', which was a confirmation that something really transpired at the outing. 'And you?' she asked, and I also replied, 'yes'. The most fascinating feature was the true revelation of her intelligence, as the first few words rolled out of her unidentified ethnic tongue. We ordered some drinks and chatted for some time. It was time to leave, and I decided to settle the bill. But that beautiful personality prevented me from paying, and she honoured the bill herself. This was something impressive. However, she was right because I was conveyed into the inn by her. Amie was admirable! We dispersed. She went home, and I moved home as well. We then started chatting more happily, as we were no longer in suspense. She was very nice and intelligent, and we became very intimate.

At the start of the following academic year, I had a physical discourse with my Dean, who intimated to me that my application had to go through the University Senate for approval before I could register. I went home disappointed, and in few days, I received a letter, verifying my reinstatement. I was in the intermediate year of the old yearly-examinations system, but on my return, a modular system had been instituted in which we wrote two semester-examinations - one in the First Semester and the other in the Second Semester. Prior to registration, Dr. Bah invited me to his office, and on my arrival, he asked: 'Samuel, you were in the Intermediate year, but we now have a modular system. The problem at hand is what year to place you?' I replied, 'Sir, you evaluate my record and place me in the equivalent year'. I was registered in the second year of the modular system, which was the equivalent of the Intermediate year. In second year, we offered courses which included Applied Electricity, Electronics Engineering, Materials and Structures, Engineering Drawings, Applied Mechanics, Thermofluids, Workshop Technology and Mathematics.

As we commenced lectures, the Quimanora club invited me to their ranks. Initially, I declined, because their initiation process was very rigid. But there were lots of friends of mine in that club, like Shabad, who succeeded in persuading me into their membership. I had another student friend, Bola, who was also a member of Quimanora. When I just started my Engineering course, we met at a birthday party at Wilberforce, the western part of Freetown. I took a girlfriend, Toma, with me. And during the party, another boy attacked me, protesting Toma was his girlfriend. But the girl was so attached to me, as if she was propelled to trigger a permanent adhesion. She continually defended our bond, displaying her unconditional passion for me. Bola and I never knew each other, but he stepped in to fortify my defence, as the boy and his friends ganged up against me. I used my father's green Mercedes-Benz 230E to get to the party and, as the situation became uncontrollable, Bola advised I go home. Together with Toma, I jumped into the car and drove off. But during the journey, I looked through my driving mirror and viewed a Mercedes-Benz, similar to mine, at top speed. Initially, I thought the guy was in a hurry heading elsewhere. But as we drove, I realized it was the boy who challenged about Toma that was chasing us. Immediately, I increased the percentage of my throttle position to maintain a good distance apart. As we wriggled, it was only The Almighty God who saved us because we almost got toppled, repeatedly negotiating road bends. Even when I arrived home, they jumped out of their vehicle and advanced towards me with an axe. They only retreated, and disappeared, when my father rushed out of our house. Since that incident, Bola became my friend. He liked me so much and also greatly influenced my invitation to Quimanora.

As an initiate you were referred to as 'Q-Borbor'. The initiation process started with a pre-initiation phase, which in some cases lasted for months depending on the situation on campus, as University regulations and other factors sometimes influenced it. Our heads were thoroughly shaved, eyebrows and beards removed as a mark of identification. We were also nicknamed. My nickname was 'Soriba yuba yase, E.T. Ormorlae worwor alias mishelin karozin dros, just added Kpanabome'. That was my Q-name as an initiate. During the pre-initiation period, initiates were faced with lots of degrading activities. On campus, members continually organized sessions in their dormitories where Q-Borbors were tortured in different ways. Sometimes, we were physically beaten. Other times we performed physical exercises, and compelled to carry out embarrassing practices. In some cases, we got isolated in closed environments like wardrobes. There was a situation in which me and some other fellow initiates were captured and conveyed into a room in the male hostel. Almost every member knew I don't smoke. So, I was forced to take a few inhalation of a stick of cigarette and dropped some lit extras in a wardrobe. Another initiate and I were then locked up in that terribly dark, smoked compartment for minutes, where I almost got myself fainted. My eyes were as red as the oozing blood of a newly-slaughtered mammal. I began hitting the closed cubicle until the ever-productive radiation from the sun's orbit slowly enveloped us. Swiftly, I jumped out of the structure and found myself partially doped on the floor. In some cases, members on campus harassed initiates financially. Some demanded expensive items that drove some initiates into activities beyond their status. But those who were considerate made moderate demands. However, that practice was a routine and you were considered a financial giant when you joined that organization. Those events continued on a daily basis, until the final day of initiation. In another instance, a fake marriage ceremony was organized between one of my then squadis, Kojo, and I. In that arrangement, I played the wife, and my colleague the husband. We swapped single shoes, wrongly dressed, and Kojo was asked to hold on to my right arm as we walked across the usually packed-full 'Bustic' – an area with a huge tree around the centre of campus, where students from different faculties and social backgrounds converged. In most cases, students of identical camps or social clubs assembled in teams. On that day, if my will was prodigal, I could have traded whatever it took to retrieve it and utilize meaningfully. But even my insular walking inclination, could not get me an escape route. Other students screamed as they witnessed that scene. To wrap that up, I was ordered to carry a tray on my head with a bottle, advertising the sale of beer, even though I preached against alcoholism. That was the most humiliating activity I ever experienced during my pre-initiation. The Quimanora initiation process had no set standards, so members designed according to their mental capabilities and torturing desires. The last of the pre-initiation events that almost triggered my ceding was when some past members arrived on campus few days to the final initiation event.

Cyclades had a party that night and some members invited me and Poopi - one of my then 'squadis'. We knew the implications, but they convinced us we were safe, and those were guys we trusted so much. Towards midnight, they received us and as we walked across 'Stone', we realized that the initial love expressed by our trusted seniors was nothing less than a brilliant set-up. As a pre-initiation criterion, initiates were obliged to pay constant visits to past members. Some past members treated you as brothers, but others man-handled you as their worst enemies. They would treat you callously. And on top of that, they would ask you to carry out laundry, and perform menial work that would get you really exhausted. I was lazy in terms of domestic work, and, in fact, visiting people was not part of my propensity. So I stayed away. Generally, I did not visit past members. But many students on campus accused me of pride. Actually, I was that introvert type, who sometimes needed time just to himself. I think deeply. That night, J-bat pulled out a whipping rod from underneath his shirt and maliciously hit me with some lashes at random. Later, he was joined by Knox and they carried me and Poopi to the famous 'Stone'. On the ground, in a sitting position, our legs were out-stretched, and Knox and J-bat quenched lit cigarettes on both shins of my legs, until they appeared as if they had just been moved over a complicated furnace. Whenever they hit my shins, I would cover them up with my hands. But that was followed by double slaps on my jaws. So I was afraid to get my hands off my jaws and the repeated hits got me frustrated. J-bat then constantly hit my damaged shins with a Coca-Cola bottle to a point I could take no more. I grabbed him in a fight, with my shins in agony, as I was no more interested in his Quimanora affair. But Bobson, one of the Enjoyers I had great respect for, arrived just at the right time and succeeded in getting me to a point of calm. I wept like a three-month old baby, yearning for breast milk. I never wanted to continue that initiation after that horrifying experience, but Bobson was able to get me continued. I went to 'Vietnam' in battered shins!

On the final day of initiation, we were garnered on campus, at about 18:00 hours, just in front of 'Stone' region and members continued minor torture, as we sang songs of Quimanora and got ready for the last touch. Campus was overcrowded, as non-Quimanora students hungrily waited to see our final trooping. We queued-up in our black jeans and white tops, and every initiate allocated a unique number, representing the order of arrival in the queue, hence 'Vietnam', as members and past-members waited on the receiving end. We were number-tagged around our upper arms, biceps and triceps region, with black cloths and numbers printed with white. When you're number one, it meant you entered first, which implied you got the 'best' of everything because members were fully energetic. Slaps, kicks, and different sorts of assault were released from members because they also lined-up on either side as you entered 'Vietnam', in readiness. In our squad, Brian was number-one, followed by D'Mills. I was still in pain as a result of my bruised shins, though I received small torture, especially around my stomach region, so my number was high. That was sensible, as they wanted members to get partially-fatigued before I stepped in. But some members were Robotic-like. They hardly got tired during that process. In my days, 'Vietnam' was located around the Engineering Faculty, well protected by members of Quimanora to prevent intruders from monitoring. In fact Elens, boys who were not members of Quimanora, and Josifins, non-Deflosacs girls, were even afraid to come close because they knew the Quimanora initiation was no kid thing. The singing and minor torture continued until just before night fell and Q-Borbors moved in a single file towards 'Vietnam'. Sometimes, in abnormal situations like Moratorium, 'Vietnam' was relocated outside the University campus, to evade disciplinary actions. The Q-initiation was difficult to stop! The process was tough, rough, harsh - I can't say! We stayed in 'Vietnam' for hours. We intensely went through almost everything we did during the pre-initiation, as if it were a form of preparation for the final date. Members sometimes fought because in some situations, a guy could protect an initiate that another guy might want to attack. This sometimes cropped-up when initiates put up a bad attitude during pre-initiation, or in other cases, a member and initiate could be rivals in a girl affair, or some other personal feud. During the first stage, I was physically protected by Powershake, or else my initiation could have been a commemorative disaster. It was carried out in stages, which represented different levels of torture. At the final stage, my mate was Haj and, relentlessly, I was transformed into a 'Q-man': an 'Enjoyer', as a member of Quimanora was referred to.

The 'Deflosacs', the female wing of Quimanora, simultaneously ran through their own initiation. It was somehow synonymous to the Quimanora initiation process, but the difference was – it was a girl thing. We all converged around Bustic, which marked the end of the initiation, and a welcome to the Q-flo business. I could remember hugging Michaela Conteh, just after the initiation process. Michaela was my Q-flo-squadi and the first Deflo-babe to hug me just after the initiation process. Michaela and I were very close, even before university. Our tie started when we both became members of the Diogramix Club. 'Toway', as we used to call each other, slowly replaced our biological nomenclature whenever we engaged in a chat or saw each other. Quimanora was eminent. It was outstanding in both camps, on campus and outside Fourah Bay College. Q had selection standards - you had to be funky and from at least an average background to be invited. They needed the best of the best. So, you never expected a membership invite if you're not in that category. As Enjoyers, we interacted with top levels of girls on campus like those of the Deflosacs, Dahlia, Elegance, Azalea and Syramax. Those girls were really beautiful and classy, and even those not that beautiful were really cute, so recognizing their ugly state was almost impossible.

Succeeding our Quimanora initiation, my bond became stronger with Amie and realized she was a member of an organization that was established in April 2002/03 academic year, under the lead of the late Jassie with Eddinia as Vice. It was formed by a group of young ladies, who decided to exclude themselves from the traditional practices of other social clubs at that time. Driven by their male wing, the Klymax Club, the group was later named Syramax. Syra represents Syraph – an angel of a high rank, and max – the suffix of Klymax. I had a junior friend called Banya. He was a member of the Klymax club, which opposed the activities of Quimanora, but we were very close and he knew almost everything about my social life. The Syraph was the most powerful member - the head of Syramax. The objective of Syramax was to cultivate young ladies into decent successful citizens. But some others believed it was a strategy of the Black Camp to win more girls into their membership. To entice young ladies into their fold, members of Syramax preached the club's vision to freshmen and were consequently invited to meetings. The aim of such meetings was to test the moral values of the new University entrants, including patience. Sometimes, joint fun-sessions were organized together with their male counterparts Klymax, meant to reinforce the relationship between the two clubs. Before an invitee could be registered as a member, an inauguration ceremony was organized in which initiates took an oath. Some of their activities within the year included the Bustic display of all interested invitees, annual cocktail party outing, with Bob-a-job prior to the cocktail party and outing. Amie, who occupied the seat of the Syraph in the 2003/04 academic year, worked very hard to a point that her club almost became the leading female organization on campus. However, her efforts were continually frustrated by the rivalry of Deflosacs, which was considered the most prominent female-student social club both on and off campus. Amie was brilliant and friendly, and her extra beauty made classy 'freshgirls' attracted to her. She was also a member of the Dahlia club, but Dahlia (which was the leading female black club) appeared to be her second priority. Amie's very successful tenure earned her another year of rule, which controlled the affairs of the Syramax club for two consecutive academic years. Syramax then became arch-rivals of Deflosacs, although Deflo was supreme. Amie later became Vice President of Fourah Bay College Student Union, under the Leadership of Solomon Jamiru, in the 2004/05 academic year. I believe Solomon Jamiru is one of the best presidents Fourah Bay College Student Union has ever produced. And his teaming with Amie offered an excellent presidential package.

As an Enjoyer, you always had the urge towards revenge during initiation. Those practices, sometimes, led to deplorable effects. My inauguration into Quimanora was really persecuting, but I never thought of any form of 'hit back' at initiates. I was muscular, with big protruding biceps and triceps, because I was into body-building, so was afraid to actively participate in initiation processes, especially physical torture by hand. But in a particular pre-session on campus, some of my fellow Enjoyers captured some Q-borbors and asked me to join them. Normally, I acted as a Moderator - to calm down other members as they carried on with initiation. But as the process continued, that day, I was tempted to get just a taste of it. Without exerting much force, I tersely slapped one of the initiates and suddenly, blood oozed out of one of his ears. He screamed in pain as I tried to calm him, but he couldn't take it and never showed up again. That was the end of his Quimanora training. He never became an Enjoyer.

Quimanora and Deflosacs were like 'true biological siblings', in spite of the fact that opposite sexes, in some cases, dated one another – 'incest' could not be prevented. Sometimes, even when a student went through difficult times, either academic or otherwise, he hardly got a feel of it because Quimanora and Deflosacs activities were always full of fun- there was always laughter involved! The interaction of Quimanora and Deflosacs were always centred on a popular bench-mark designated 'Stone'.

*

The Stone

The popular 'stone' was the point of convergence of members of the Quimanora club, and hence Deflosacs, located on Fourah Bay College campus. It was approximately 20m from the 'helipad', the location where students and others picked a cab to move down town and elsewhere. In reality, 'the stone' composed of a concrete step, supported by lumps of granite stones, mortared together. From morning to evening, 'Stone' was full of different sets of 'Enjoyers' and 'Deflo-babes', at different times, having fun – as dictated by lecture, and personal study, timetables. Sometimes, we relaxed to an extent that we didn't want to go home. Resident students, most times, stayed there up to late in the night. Some went to their dormitories to sort things out, before returning to 'Stone'. We never got tired of being at 'Stone', except for academic and other social reasons. There was something about that 'Stone' I couldn't explain. Even students who were not members of Q and Deflo liked hanging around 'Stone'. Quimanora were just fascinating, but always worked with their female counterparts, Deflosacs. Elens always wanted to get affiliated with Q in order to share that glory. Even 'Josifins' did not only want to identify with Enjoyers and Deflo-babes, but wanted to date Enjoyers, just to get a feel of them. When we had parties, it was like a political campaign in which other students lobbied for invites. They believed you were only respected or high-class when considered in the 'Q-flo business'. This then, made the 'Stone' not only a meeting point of Q and Deflo, but also of Elens and Josifins interested in Q-flo affairs, though they were only allocated limited time there; you were not permitted to stay there long when you were not part of Quimanora or Deflosacs. Even if you delayed, you became uncomfortable as you would be unintentionally isolated, because you would not be a party to discussion. 'Stone' was a Q-flo thing!

During the annual athletic sports meet at Fourah Bay College, we installed a musical set with speakers of very high decibel output, at 'Stone', with mild drinks and liquors. A good number of us didn't show up for the actual sporting activities, at Havloc ground, except for participants and a few supporters. We danced all day, carousing with our Deflo-babes, girlfriends and other loyal friends, as others rushed to the Havloc ground in support of their Davidson Nicol, Solomon Caulker and Bai Bureh Hall Participants. But most of the non-participating Quimanora members celebrated the athletic encounter at 'Stone'.

*

We wrote the two semester examinations and I got promoted to the third year of my Engineering course. In our faculty, we had three departments; Civil, Mechanical/Maintenance, and Electrical and Electronics Engineering. I was interested in the Electrical department and was qualified, so I opted for the Electrical and Electronics Engineering discipline. In our department, we offered courses which included Electronics, Electrical Circuits/Fields, Microcomputer Engineering, Power Engineering, Communications, Digital Systems and Mathematics. The course was rough and tough, but with hard work, you stopped at nothing to emerge successful. It was time for the first semester examinations and the timetable was posted, as usual. There was contention on one of our modules. Communications I was set for 16th July,

2004, but was postponed to 27th July of the same year. It kept alternating between these two dates until a consensus was reached to maintain that subject for 27th July. Officially, the first module on the timetable was supposed to be a Mathematics module, set for July 17th. I was non-resident, so I stayed at home, doing my final revision. I left home on 16th July, at about 16:00 hours, to get ready for my supposed first examination, which was my usual practice. I resided on campus on the eve of my first paper. About an hour later, I arrived and met some of my colleagues of a different faculty at the entrance of the male Davidson Nicol hostel. We were very much familiar, playing and joking, and one of them, Samuel Bondi, uttered 'are you just arriving?' I replied 'yes'. He continued, 'your classmates took Communications I this morning, you don't offer it, do you?' I replied, 'in my department, all third year students offer the same and all modules.' He emphasized, 'well, they've taken it already'. I treated it trivially, as I thought it was a normal joke, but yelled 'stop that nonsense'. He did input some more seriousness and vowed to his Bachelor's in the making, then I realized it was something realistic. He was in the Civil Engineering Department. Suddenly, I dropped my luggage on the floor and ran to my closest classmate's room. Dominic During was my classmate since sixth form, which made our bond stronger. Fortunately, he was in. As soon as he set an eye on me, his facial expression transformed, manifesting sentiment. He knew I was not in the examination hall and came to verify. Dominic couldn't say a word, he just handed a question paper to me, which read 'First Semester Examination for the Degree of BEng in Electrical and Electronics Engineering, Year III, Communications I, 2004'. That was the first time I wept due to academic predicament. He tried consoling me, but there was nothing he could do, as the situation could not be reversed. The implication was, when you missed or failed a module, you automatically repeated the academic year - there were no retake examinations. I ran to my Head of Department and tried to explain, but he couldn't listen. I approached the lecturer in charge of that module, Dr. Joseph Kanu, who gave me audience because he knew it could've happened to any student. He further explained that the decision was made on 15th July, to set that examination for the 16th again. Of course, he wasn't supportive of the change. He offered me a word of consolation, and encouraged me to take the remaining modules. My friend, Dominic, also explained he tried to contact me on phone, but that my phone was switched off. Yes, he was right because I, most times, turned off my cell phone during final revision, to evade distraction. He knew my residence, but according to him, he only got the news at about 23:00 hours on 15th July, and there was no cab to carry him. Some other friends wanted to contact me, but didn't, because they thought Dominic had informed me already. The psychological effect rained on me as I read for the remaining papers; I had no good concentration, but decided to be strong. I wrote the remaining papers and made good grades, with incomplete grade points due to the deletion of Communications I.

We commenced the second semester and hard work started, as usual. Again, it was time for examinations. I wrote all modules, and made good grades, with an 'F' in Electronics II. Electronics II was not that difficult, but approximately sixty percent of the class got 'Fs'. Well, our then-Lecturer of that Electronics Course, Mr. Bangura, contested a Councillor Election. That Lecturer was in a bad relationship with many students and only started befriending when he had a political intention. During his campaign, especially in his Lecture periods, he repeatedly admonished us to register around campus, which was his region, and vote for him. Deceptively, we agreed, and when it was time for the elections, most of us travelled to our various homes, ignoring his expected balloting. He disgracefully lost the election and became bitter towards us, so the questions he set during the examination were deeper than expected. Even some who made passing grades were somehow questionable. However, I repeated the academic year, not just because of Electronics II, but because of my absence in Communications I, so I had two modules against, as single Fs were given concession.

I spent two years in third-year. The first year I refer to as 'Lower third-year' and the second year as 'Upper third-year'. In the first semester of my upper third-year, I offered Electrical Circuits together with Communications I and succeeded in both, in preparation for another semester of work.

■■■

CHAPTER IV

Exterminating Attempts

My life as a student could have ended by hidden methodologies, as I struggled to maintain my academic vision.

In the second semester of my lower third year, a friendly Soccer match was set between Cyclades and Paciphix clubs. These two were junior social clubs of the White Camp at Fourah Bay College. In most cases, 'Freshboys', boys who had just entered Fourah Bay College, got initiated into these two male clubs before being invited to join the Quimanora membership. So, most Enjoyers were either members of Cyclades or the Paciphix club, as well. These two were internal rivals in the White Camp, even though they displayed true love for each other at the Quimanora level. They fought to win initiates, especially at the start of the academic year. And whenever they met on a junior-club basis, either side wanted to exhibit supremacy, but the Quimanora bond kept them together. The Paciphix club were more violent in their operation, as opposed to 'Happy-men' – the members of Cyclades. The Paciphix behavioural procedures were closely related to that of their parent social club, Quimanora, especially regarding their initiation process, whilst Cyclades were more gentlemanly. So whenever those two junior clubs clashed, either side wanted to prove he was the 'big brother'.

The Soccer match was hosted at the Havloc ground, during which I played my usual wing - number nine. Other non-playing members and non-members interested not just in the Match, but in the Quimanora, and hence Cyclades and Paciphix affairs, were sometimes around to display their support. In my days, I was outstanding in whatever match I was involved in, whether friendly or not. The kick-off was whistled and the struggle started. As the match continued, you could see that both sides were really determined to carry the victory. You could see constructive dribbling, good passes, shots on target and brilliant saves by goalkeepers. Many of us were exposed to Soccer during primary and secondary school days, which made the match very interesting. That game was a real battle, as we were deep into the second half, still nil-nil. A few minutes before the end of the match, I was upset and very hungry for a goal. My mates knew me very well. They knew what I was capable of doing when thirsty to score. Suddenly, I received a nice pass from one of my team players. I dribbled through three players of the opposing team, and was challenged by the last defender, Zinho. Zinho was very tall, over 6ft. I made a few moves to bypass him, but he was a good defender and very stubborn. Also, he knew if I beat him, the only option would be a goal against them, ensuring their defeat. At a point, I devised another strategy, pretended to sail the ball between his legs and as he got distracted downwards, I raised the ball above and over his head, in spite of his lengthy phenotype. In our local dialect, krio, we referred to that move as 'Popor-rep'. Successfully, I bypassed him and moved forward, but the ball was still above my shoulder, as Zhino was very tall. So I decided to give the ball a head for proper positioning to take a good shot into the goal, as the goalkeeper had been displaced already. Shockingly, I felt something on my head that instantly took me out of my lucidity. It was Zhino's leg on my face. I dropped to the ground and, for about fifteen minutes, my human senses were obliterated. My pupil and iris turned white, as they rolled in pain, and friends were scared, thinking they were going to lose me. With water poured all over me, I regained consciousness, and was carried home. I looked normal, but in the morning, my affected right eye was really distended. I was conveyed to an optician who put me on some medication. When the inflammation disappeared, I had problems with my sight, and a pair of glasses recommended. For the rest of the semester, right through the examinations, that pair of spectacles became my crony. I don't like eye-aids and was very uncomfortable with it. After the second-semester exams, I decided to drop it, and God helped me, my vision greatly improved. There was no need for an artificial optical helper. I took the second semester examinations and we vacated. Simultaneously, my former study-mate, Ishmael Lisk, was rounding up his Electrical and Electronics Engineering course. He successfully completed as the best student of his class, with first class honours. I was so proud of him because he dedicatedly pursued and achieved his merited dream.

    As a student, sometimes I was resident, but for most of my days I was non-resident. During my resident phases, I usually went home at weekends, and returned to campus on Sunday evenings. Sometimes, my father's driver would take me to campus, but other times, I picked up a cab. One Sunday evening, I left home for campus, by taxi, and arrived at Model Junction. There were some students waiting for the college bus, and some of us were in queue for taxis. At one particular time, I was second in the queue; on the left side of the taxi rank, since they parked on the right hand side of the street, awaiting passengers to fill in. Another boy was in front of me, but whether he was a student, I couldn't tell. Suddenly, I heard the sound of a fire engine from a distance. Within minutes, the vehicle appeared in view from the lower end of Circular Road, a road that led to Model Junction, and ran across it. The vehicle swayed in our direction with a non-stopping speed. In my mind, I closely followed the trajectory of that firefighting vehicle and realized it was on the wrong path. Something mysteriously moved me and I started running with a very high, abnormal velocity. Everybody was laughing because they couldn't comprehend my analysis. The vehicle was faster than I could run and, suddenly, a force I couldn't explain pulled me up and over that taxi and laid me on the ground, on the right hand side of the parked taxi. The boy, who stood before me, in the queue, remained in the same position. In seconds, the fire engine hit him with a force he couldn't resist, and he was thrown approximately ten metres away. He couldn't talk, he couldn't cry, he couldn't walk! People around looked at me with eyes of comprehension, and then they realized what was going on. They acknowledged it was only The All-Powerful God who preserved my life. The boy lay on the ground helplessly. The vehicle didn't even stop, as that was their normal practice on mission. That became another discussion on campus. I ran to campus and the boy was later conveyed to the hospital. A few days later, his death was rumoured, though I didn't verify because I did no follow-up. I was full of fear.

In the upper third-year second semester, in March, my father arrived from a vacation in London. He was using a Mercedes-Benz saloon car, but decided to get a four-wheel drive, as he needed to be travelling to the provinces. Freeman and I sought and were able to get a black Pathfinder. Dad was over seventy years old then and only went out on special appointments. So the Sports Utility Vehicle was at my disposal and I used it often. In that second semester, I offered only two modules, which earned me lots of time for fun. Sometimes, I used that vehicle to go to parties, night clubs, campus and other activities. In the first semester, the Q-flo initiation was in progress and something cropped up. I identified one of the initiates of Deflosacs. She was very beautiful, with features I admired. I didn't talk with her, at that point, but had a chat with one of the Deflo-babes. She informed me that a number of boys were after her, but remained resistant. I didn't hesitate and was prepared to face the fight, as I didn't want to let her go. I received her cell phone number from Hafsatu – a Deflo-babe - who advised me to consult her for help if I encountered any challenge. I gave Aisha a call and we made an appointment for the next day evening. That year, I spent less time at 'stone', considering my academic repetition, so she didn't know I was an 'Enjoyer'. She was a 'Freshgirl'. She was resident, and the next day, at about 17:00 hours, I knocked at her door and this beautiful figure opened. The first reception was her brilliant smile, affirming her commitment to my continued visits. Her whitish teeth just matched the jester-like characteristic she slowly manifested. I entered and was offered a comfortable sitting position on her bed. She was in her room, together with her roomie, both of whom offered me a red-carpet welcome. Aisha was wrapping up her spaghetti and meat dinner preparation. She dished some out and we ate together. Normally, I didn't eat at a stranger's, except for very close friends and relations, but yielded to her offer as a form of romantic accommodation. I discussed nothing about my Quimanora involvement, but she informed me of her being a Deflo-initiate and would be having a session that night. The session was a Santigie - an event in which Quimanora and Deflosacs initiates met, exchanged ideas, danced to bubu-music, sometimes preceded or accompanied by other initiation exercises. It was all fun! The Deflo-initiate asked me to be back at night and promised to give a call after the meeting. I smiled and replied, 'okay'. The session started. Q-Borbors and Deflo-Titis were dancing on campus to the bubu-music. At about two hours' later, it was dark and I arrived. I started dancing, moving around the initiates as usual. My eyes caught that pretty figure, as she rolled her protruding hips, but didn't bother her as other boys were troubling her, busy whispering in her ears... what? I couldn't figure it out, and didn't want to expose my hidden mission. But, as I was moving past her, she caught my T-shirt, quickly pulled me backwards and closer to her. She whispered, 'why didn't you tell me you're an Enjoyer?' I smiled and she continued, 'I need some water'. She was very thirsty, as they'd danced for hours. I couldn't find water, but bought her an ice-cold orange drink: Fanta. Some, I poured into her mouth until she was truly satisfied and did the same to all other Deflo-Titis, to avoid suspicion. Later, I secretly delivered chewing gum into her hand for endurance, and to help keep her breath fresh. The session ended, but I hung around friends at 'Stone'. As soon as she got into her room, I received a phone call, demanding my immediate presence. I went there and spent a few minutes because I had to go home. That was the beginning of our relationship!

Aisha completed her initiation process, and with Lady-bird Ballay as head, she became active in the affairs of Quimanora and Deflosacs - who were notorious for three forms of traditional parties - Forces, Dashes and Clashes.

Forces

'Forces' was an event organized by Quimanora, not too long after the initiation process, as a form of welcoming new members. That was a very hot party in which Q-men dressed in ladies' attire. It was real fun, as girls invited us to their dormitories – at Lati Hyde and Beethoven – for make-up as we moved around their hostels. Lati Hyde-Forster was the first female graduate of Fourah Bay College and the first female

African school principal in Sierra Leone. In some cases, distinguishing between male and female became much more difficult as we all put on similar clothing, particularly for some of us who were somehow handsome and not hairy. 'Forces' was strictly a Q-flo thing; no Elen, no Josifin! Even Deflo-babes, whose boyfriends were Enjoyers, were not allowed to attend. This was a maddening practice, because some Enjoyers 'hooked up' with other Deflo-babes when their girlfriends were not around, but the constitution had to be maintained. Sometimes, members cunningly tried to violate that rule as a result of not trusting their partners, but when caught, you faced the required consequence.

Dashes

'Dashes' was a form of Forces, but hosted by Deflosacs. In this, we all dressed normally. Boys dressed like boys and girls like girls. Similarly, Enjoyers with Deflo girlfriends were forbidden to attend. The exclusion of Enjoyers, in Dashes, sometimes posed some menace. Some Enjoyers were very jealous, and didn't trust their sweethearts and other Enjoyers. However, it was all as a result of deep love. Some members, sometimes, did not allow their lovers to attend parties they were not mandated to attend. For instance, when it was time for Dashes, an Enjoyer could decide not to allow his Deflo-partner to be a part. Well, constitutionally, it was wrong, but relationship rights were also respected, though those arrangements were private; they were not, officially, to the knowledge of the clubs.

Clashes

The Q-flo thing was like a real mystery! 'Elen n Josifin dem nor bin undastand' – 'Elens and Josifins did not comprehend'. 'Clashes' was the real thing. As the name implies, it was an event in which Quimanora and Deflosacs 'clashed'. This was a party hosted by Q and Deflo, so the full membership was present - no exemptions. Whether you had a sweetie in the opposite club or not, whether you had a 'yuji' or not, you were all entitled to be present. 'Yuji' was a tag for 'secret lover'. In other words, you could be a recognized partner of someone else, but somebody else was dating you in secret. I remember that, at a particular time, I was dating two Deflo-babes - Aisha and Pat. Aisha was recognized and Pat in the dark. I loved Aisha so much, but had started falling in with Pat. So, in one of our parties, I posed with Pat, in a corner I thought Aisha would not know. Surprisingly, Aisha just walked up to me, demanding I go and get her a drink. My goodness! That night, I almost disowned my true identity. I looked at Aisha in the eye, and realized rejection would transform her friendly emotions into a non-loving characteristic. She was caring! But I could sense a girl ever-determined to achieve a demand, especially in the case of internal rivalry. A Q-friend, Aziz, was just by me and offered me a smiling stare, which explained, 'they would deal with you tonight, because you're too much'. Aisha was a Deflo-babe and service, at the bar, was open to all. How could she ask me to go and get her a drink from the bartender? It was an embarrassing situation. She only did to get me off her mate. But yes, I dated her first, and she had all rights to any form of reasonable demand. Pat was cool, and I also made a request to move to the bar, which she approved. However, I got a drink, which Aisha accepted. That night was bitter for me. I couldn't enjoy it as much as usual. The most upsetting event was when it was time for home. Both girls demanded I take them home; I was using my father's black Pathfinder. So I carried the two of them in a single vehicle, together with their friends. However, I dropped them at their respective homes. Clashes, I believe, were the 'hottest' campus party hosted by Quimanora and Deflosacs. In the first 'Clashes' I ever attended, as a new Enjoyer, something very interesting happened. Normally, I don't take alcohol! I am teetotal! Most of my friends and club-mates were aware of that fact, but I believed they decided to play a game with me. Secretly, I believe, they informed the bartender not to offer me any non-alcoholic drink. Every time I went, he would say there's no more soft drink, even though I saw other people getting them from the bar. I was pushed to the wall, very thirsty as I used to dance a lot, and decided to imbibe some beer to sate my appetite. I took a single can of Carlsberg, poured it through my oesophagus and felt somehow satisfied. Normally, I used to dance a lot, but that time I was very bold. In minutes, I started viewing dimmed images. Then, I started walking slowly and was on the floor, right on stage. I got intoxicated. I was drunk! I could sense and see people pulling down my boxer shorts, but couldn't figure them out, let alone stop them, as I lost complete control of myself. I woke up in the morning, in Kojo's room – on campus. Kojo informed me that some Deflo-babes were trying to pull down my boxer short, but were prevented from doing so by him. 'Clashes' were a big Q-flo thing.

Quimanora and Deflosacs also organized off-campus end-of-year events, but at most times independently. These events were normally held during the holidays, which I, many times, attended with a Quimanora-friend 'Old-Skool'. Deflo organized parties, fashion shows and other social activities. I could remember one of the beach outings organized by Deflo, in which my then off-campus girlfriend and her friends clashed with Nadia Kamara and her friends. On my return to the University, I had two close female friends – Blessing and Nadia. Blessing was a Civil Engineering student.

But she was born-again, so didn't attend most of our social club functions, which made our friendship weaker. Nadia was a member of Deflosacs, which strengthened our friendship. Nadia and my off-campus lover used to fight on the phone, as my then-sweetheart was very jealous of her. So when I arrived at the outing together with my girlfriend, and her friends, Nadia saluted me with a tap on my hand. My girlfriend knew her by face, and she responded in a manner Nadia didn't support, which led to the oral confrontation. To maintain peace, I couldn't enjoy the outing. I just took my girlfriend and her friends away from that event. Sometimes, Quimanora organized barbeques, other times beach outings. But one of the most remarkable and memorable of the end-of-year events hosted was the two-consecutive-day party initiated by a former chief of Quimanora club - Abu-kai, also known as Buski. I enjoyed parties, but that was somehow unprecedented. We enjoyed the first night, went home, and returned for the second night. It was hectic, as some got tired for the second day, but we endured. Past members, a major wing of Quimanora and Deflosacs, were very supportive, respected and not exempt from those parties.

Early one afternoon, I didn't have lectures and decided to take a ride to campus, with one of my younger sisters, Alima, in the front seat. Alima was the first child and only daughter Dad had with Isatu, and was really fond of me. We arrived on Fourah Bay College campus and I decided to see my darling Aisha, at the Lati Hyde hostel. My baby sister, Alima, was left in the vehicle and I headed to the dormitory. I spent some time with Aisha and she asked me to drop her home, at her residence, for a weekend break. She energetically walked out of her room, with her normally long braided natural hair that offered her the distinct Fulani look, sweeping off any intruding particle as it waved around her beautiful face. Well, she was not that focused on physical body maintenance, as her huge phenotype was naturally accommodating, but hopping in and out of her Lati Hyde dormitory, compensated for any loss of life-long exercises. Aisha took the back seat, leaving my sister in front. It was even. We were off and it started raining. Normally, my siblings and I didn't use seatbelts, but Alima did that day. I tried asking her to take it off, but she maintained it. She did not remove it. I dropped my girlfriend at her residence and headed back for home. It was about 21:00 hours! On our way back, we made a stop to see one of my stepsisters, Fatmata, who was residing with a family friend, Ola, Uncle Kabbia's daughter, at Wellington – a locale in the east end of Freetown. Fatmata was a daughter of Isatu, but had a different father. Isatu had her before getting married to Dad. Fatmata and I were also very close. Approximately five minutes after leaving F.A., as we used to call Fatmata, I was at top speed. It was still raining heavily... and it was dark! Suddenly, a beam from an opposing vehicle got in my eyes. I couldn't see my way and immediately released the throttle pedal to assist my deceleration. In a few seconds, I totally lost control of the vehicle, but firmly held on to the steering wheel to prevent it from hitting my chest. I was off the road, on my left, over the slabs and started hearing all sorts of sound – 'pooh', 'boom', 'bam'... The first thought that enveloped me was 'Is this how I die?' But in a moment, I hit my head on the steering wheel and I was just inspired from within to shout the Name of Jesus. I shouted 'Jesus', for the second time 'Jesus', and the third I shouted 'Jesus'. Immediately, the vehicle was brought to a halt, hitting a metallic street electric pole. I was partially unconscious, bleeding profusely through my nose and my white shirt turned red with my own blood. I got out of the vehicle, running out of shock, but was captured by someone. As The Almighty God did it, there was a private hospital very close to the scene, where I was conveyed and admitted. When we arrived, the doctor demanded consultation fees from me, even though I was close to death. But God has uncountable ways of fixing problems, bringing His Word to pass. On my way to campus, Mum had sent me to pick up some cash on her behalf, which I did. That cash was in my pocket, which one of the nurses used to pay the consultation fees, and settled my medical bill. Nobody knew, probably without that cash, I could have bled to death, because the doctor insisted on the consultation fee before attending to me. However, he was able to stop the bleeding and put me on drips for hours. My sister was fine! She was physically saved by the seatbelt. That was a divine arrangement because even when I tried convincing her to remove it, through mockery, she remained respectfully defiant. As I was struggling with the steering wheel, I could view her being pulled backwards repeatedly to her normal position. She could've gone through the windshield, with a high probability of her head being stuck to death, but our Lord Jesus stepped in, and I give Him all Glory. Alima gave my Mum a call, who urgently arrived at the scene. When Mum saw the damaged vehicle, she was afraid to see me. She thought I had been seriously disfigured. The SUV had a very strong metal guard in front, which got truly deformed as a result of the impact. The metallic street pole also got bent downwards. The vehicle was crushed, really battered, which frightened my mother. Everyone who saw that vehicle made the same statement - 'the driver died'. And, worst of it, it collided with an electric pole. We could have been electrocuted. But Jesus stepped in. My Mum went to the hospital with a mind in turmoil. She was perplexed. She was afraid to get into my ward, but the doctor succeeded in persuading her, emphasizing that my physical state was alright. Mum cautiously walked into the ward in little steps till she viewed my total being, verifying the doctor's description: no scars, but I was still on a medical drip. Later, I was referred to the emergency hospital in Goderich, located in the outer west of Freetown, for further medical examinations. I was X-rayed by a white radiographer, a medical doctor, whose diagnosis proved the normalcy of my brain and skull. I was safe, in good shape and health. Both of the medical doctors made the same remarks; 'with the degree of accident, considering the impact, you're supposed to have a problem with your brain or skull'. Another person made a remark that it, sometimes, shows up after about six months. But it's now over a decade, with no trouble! Jesus would remain glorified!

When she got the news, Aisha tried calling me on the phone, but couldn't access me. She tried seeing me, but she couldn't, as I was being protected. When she saw me on campus, about three days after the incident, she couldn't believe it. She screamed, 'I thought there would be wounds all over you, thank God!' The Almighty God operates perfectly. Even friends and others couldn't believe I had a terrible accident. The next day, I went to Aisha's room, on campus, and displayed the picture. She shouted 'Samou', gave me a hug and reiterated that I was only saved by The Almighty God. The vehicle was removed from the scene before she went there, so that was the first time of seeing the damage.

Our Lord Jesus delivered me and I was safe.

■■■

CHAPTER V

My First Year in Final Year

Successfully, I completed the third year and got promoted to the final year of my Electrical Engineering course.

My life in final year was tough! Tuition commenced in October, as usual, and I was preparing to graduate in the 2005/06 academic year for a general Bachelor's, BEng, in Electrical and Electronics Engineering. In final year, we received tuition on courses which included Signal Analysis, Advanced Power Engineering, Control Systems, advanced Digital Systems, Data Processing, Advanced Communications Systems, Industrial Economics and Management, and Engineers in Society. The course was challenging, so I increased my study period, as this was my final year and I was more determined than ever. In spite of the tediousness, I was really enjoying the course. But as we got along, I noticed a change. I started having some form of distraction from my coursework, and gradually reduced my study time. At a point, I even forgot I was a student, as I almost neglected my academic vision. The distraction was not due to clubbing, partying or any social activity on campus, but truly related to my then-girlfriend. I always had girlfriends. I always made relationships easily, and though she was not as beautiful as other girls I dated in all forms, if I could class them, she totally gained my attention. I couldn't read my notes. I didn't go out often, but would be with her in my bedroom all day. Sometimes, I spent lots of time at her residence, and we hardly discussed anything related to academia.

It was about two weeks to the commencement of the first semester examinations and I thought about separating from my girlfriend until after the examinations. Implementing that inner proposal was more than a Herculean task, as living without her was like a heartbreaking exercise. It was like our souls were intertwined, and nothing could separate them. I started dilly-dallying, and sometimes studying in her bedroom, but my parents' pressure on me was on the increase, as they recognised her as a distracting element. Detaching from her was a real battle, which only a resilient mind could win. I left her for that period, but not wholeheartedly. A week to the examinations, in the final year, but I had not been reading effectively! What could I write with incomplete notes? I am intelligent, but no matter how brilliant you might be, you need hard work to genuinely get you through a University, or any tertiary examination. I liaised with my classmates and completed about 90% of our lecture notes. Then I made a resolution to fully concentrate on my examinations, repelling my distraction, for that duration. I didn't reside on campus for that examination, as I needed time just to myself. I was way behind, and wanted to be totally focused and capture what I could. I began working, but working on seven Electrical and Electronics modules in final-year was not a job for children. I couldn't run through all of them! So I designed a strategy, which I believed could be a recipe for the examinations. I scanned through the modules, and decided to handle them in order of occurrence on the posted examinations timetable, in keeping with my acquired knowledge.

At some point during the first semester, my father's first wife, Mrs. Nancy Koroma, travelled to Freetown after a long stay in London. She had migrated to the United Kingdom, where she lived with some of her children including Andy, Bialo, Suba and Jorbay. Grandma Nancy, Ngor Nancy, or Mama Nancy as she was commonly known, got involved in an accident, in London, on her way to a usual Friday prayer meeting - she was a Muslim. From family reports, she was about to climb into a moving bus, because she was a bit late, but couldn't make it; she slipped, and in seconds was on the ground, screaming in excruciating pain. Grandma Nancy was hospitalized, administered the required medical treatment and discharged. On recovery, she decided to get back home in preparation for a permanent stay. Not too long afterwards, she was sick, and admitted at the LAC clinic, located along Syke Street, Freetown. We used to pay her regular visits to help in the healing process and pay loyalty. On a Sunday, in February, we were at the hospital, together with some of my siblings, but I left for home in the evening, at about 1800 hours, to do my final revision - getting ready for an examination on Monday morning. Almost everybody at home was at the hospital with Grandma Nancy, attending to her in various forms. At about 2100 hours, I was still on the table, in my bedroom, when I heard an unexpected knock on the door. Who was it? It was one of my step-mothers, Bintu, nick-named Glorjy. I asked, 'what is it?', because I needed time to focus on my Communications module. She replied, 'something happened'. 'What?' I responded. She intimated to me that they went to a sorcerer who revealed that somebody is responsible for Grandma Nancy's situation. I am not interested in any form of sorcery, but gave her audience to cleverly extract whatever I could from her statement. She continued, 'the sorcerer said someone, a dark personality in our family, has executed a witchcraft ritual to pass Grandma Nancy away.' Why? She couldn't explain. She continued that, according to the fetish priest, if Grandma Nancy did not pass off that night, she would never die. What was she talking about? I believed almost everybody in the family related Grandma Nancy's trouble to the accident in London, but what was Glorjy saying? I shouted 'Jesus, why?' But I didn't make a move because I remembered when I was at the hospital, Laila Najib, believed to be a strong woman of God, was there. Sister Laila was a close family friend and like a sister to my elder siblings, as they were contemporaries. At the hospital, she laid hand on Grandma Nancy, prayed for her and promised to be back at about 23:00 hours. I was not a 'true Christian'. I was still in the world, but understood spiritual principles and believed in Jesus Christ. Glorjy's disclosure was serious, but with Laila's stance, I was satisfied because I knew what Jesus could do.

Bintu departed and I continued my study. About thirty minutes later, she was back, informing me of the death of Grandma Nancy. Immediately, I jumped off the table, locked my bedroom and headed towards the hospital. As I approached the entrance, two of my elder siblings, Suba and Jorbay, who happened to be daughters of the late Grandma Nancy, were bitterly weeping, confirming their mother's expiration. Tears rained down from my eyes as I hugged my sisters in empathy. The death of Grandma Nancy was a great loss, not only to family members, but to friends as well. We wept, to a great extent – I was upset. I thought about Bintu's reports. I didn't want to unfold it to avoid domestic chaos, but couldn't help. Emotionally, I was in pain! My spirit was agitated. Grandma Nancy's death was a great loss, and how could I keep that? My sisters were in great pain, so I didn't consider them ideal for that reception. But Freeman was present. Freeman was also a son of Ngor Mamanyor – Dad's second wife – who was then based in the United States. I thought Freeman was the best person to reveal it to. I wanted my sisters to know, but in a diplomatic way, and at the right time. But sometimes, when you decide to be open, you run into predicament. Other times, when you're able to make logical decodes, you get into trouble. I am analytical and interpreted Bintu's message to Freeman. According to her declarations, the plan was to pass Grandma Nancy off under all cost that night, because if the person failed, she would never succeed. So that dark personality was really determined. Why? I couldn't tell. But Laila prayed, and promised to be back at about 23:00 hours. I believed in Jesus and was sure that, when Laila returned, Grandma Nancy could be revived and would continue in a healthy state. So I believed what they did was to cut her off before Laila's arrival. I don't believe in sorcery, but believed what Bintu said. She said that person was determined to pass Grandma Nancy off that night, and it happened. Satan has a lesser power than The Almighty God, but in terms of sorcery, his agents can also see through the supernatural, using demonic means. That message I revealed to my brother, but how he relayed it, I couldn't tell, and in the eyes of some, I appeared to be a murderer. My sisters loved me so much, and couldn't believe I had anything to do with their mother's demise. But the repeated murmurings by other relations, sometimes, set their belief in an unstable state. I was waiting for someone to face me on that issue, and then I would have explained how I knew about what I revealed to my brother, but the true reason for not confronting me is yet to be verified.

As a teenager, I had my first personal encounter with Jesus, which stabilized my conversion from Islam to Christianity. Since then, He has deposited spiritual gifts into me. Sometimes, when people discuss me negatively, our Lord Jesus reveals it to me. Grandma Nancy's death was a tremendous loss, as she was more than a mother to all of us. She was notorious for her benevolence. I could remember the nice shirt she sent me when she returned from the United Kingdom. She never distinguished between her children and others. Grandma Nancy, rest in total peace. We pray for God to offer you eternal life in Heaven - in the Name of Jesus Christ.

Grandma Nancy's death issue almost affected my first-semester examinations, especially Communications III, which I had the succeeding day. That could've been another distraction, or impeding factor, to another Communications module, but I fought to remain strong. I took the Communications III module together with the other modules, before going on vacation. When it was time for our results to be published, I was nervous and very jittery. The Results were posted and I obtained the following: B, B, C+, D, D, F, F.

It's evident I failed two modules, as D was our minimum pass grade, but considering my preparation, you can judge what could've happened if I had worked very hard from the start. For a stupid student, probably it could have been all Fs. If I could make Bs, then I was capable of making As, with good preparation.

We commenced the second semester and our then Head of Department instituted a brand new regulation. When you failed a module in the first semester, you didn't take the corresponding module in the second semester, which depicted automatic repetition. What? This could not have been a worry to me, but it was supposed to be effected in the succeeding academic year. Alternatively, we should have been notified before the first-semester examinations, at the start of the academic year. But how could you bring a new regulation in right at the start of the second semester, which was related to first semester issues, and effected it then? That was an imposition. However, we couldn't fight with it, and all of us who failed modules in the first semester examinations did not register for the corresponding modules in the second semester, and there were no reference exams. I registered for five modules, leaving out Power Engineering IV and Control Systems II, which were the corresponding second-semester modules of Power Engineering III and Control Systems I that I failed in the first semester. Tuition continued, and when we took the second semester examinations, I passed all modules, with an A in Engineers in Society (EIS), B in Data Processing and B in Communications IV. EIS was an Engineering Literature module. At one point, I was absent for a few days, and on resumption, my classmates informed me of an assignment given by our EIS Lecturer, Mr. R.A.B. Johnson, which would be used as part of our continuous assessment grades. The topics were posted, from which we were free to make our different choices. The deadline of submission was the next day and I selected the topic 'There's Need for Improvement in Engineering Training'. On arriving home, after a brief rest, I immediately started working on my paper. I listed my points on an A4-sized sheet and successfully expanded them to completion. The next day, I submitted it, and when our papers were returned by the lecturer, I obtained 23/30, which is approximately 77%. In that paper, I discussed improving the deplorable state of our Engineering Laboratory, the quality of Lecturers, including Teaching Techniques, Industrial Attachment/Internship Enhancement, and more. The highest grade I saw was 25/30, approximately 83%. And my colleague who got the 83% confessed he just Googled and all the ideas came up which he dubbed. Another colleague, Jalloh, asked where I got my points from, and I pointed to my head. He wanted to challenge me, especially when he knew I only had information about the assignment the day before the deadline, when they had already submitted. And he was the one who informed me about that assignment. But some friends who knew about my creative writing skill did not doubt me, and I was able to convince him. However, that was verified in the second-semester examinations when I got that 'A' in EIS. As we continued with academics, it was time for the student union elections.

Campus Elections

Political fight at Fourah Bay College was rough! As stated earlier, there were two major camps - the Black camp, and the White camp. They were like the Sierra Leone People's Party – SLPP, and the All People's Congress - APC, the major political parties in Sierra Leone. I believe some corrupt politicians were incubated at Fourah Bay College and nurtured downtown. The 'Generals' represented the White camp and the 'Auradicals' represented the Black camp. Both camps presented their candidates ahead of the Student Union Presidential and Senate elections. An independent candidate sometimes popped up, but the real battle was always between representatives of the Black and White camps. Student Union elections were a tough struggle, which sometimes led to violent confrontations among supporters of opposing camps.

In the process, flag-bearers together with some other executive members go around campus, organizing sessions, sensitizing fellow students with the aim of cajoling them to cast their political ballots in their favour. Campus was usually hot, which most times affected academic work, as some die-hearted supporters did not attend lectures. Some students rushed to Obelisk, which was the most expensive restaurant on campus; some ran to Fine Things, which was owned by the wife of Professor Redwood Sawyerr. Fine Things was like a convenience store in which stuff like birthday cards, food and other basic human needs were sold. Others rushed to cheaper alternatives like the 'Fry Fry' Point, where bread and other sandwiched items like fried fish, fried potatoes, fried plantain and boiled/fried eggs were sold. Some others rushed to the college Cafeterias 1, 2 and 3 to keep their digestive systems busy. I still remember the Third-world canteen.

The elections period was full of fun. There were random contentions, especially among opposing supporters, in response to their presidential candidacies. It was a period in which we analyzed speeches of Aspirants. During campaigns, sometimes students of competing camps, even those who were close friends, behaved like enemies, but reconciled when the elections period ended, for whomsoever emerged as the winner governed the student body as a whole. There were situations in which students even challenged the Police, but the law enforcement team always succeeded in bringing the situation under control.

The manifesto night, on the eve of the elections, was a night of unfolding the aims and objectives of aspiring presidents. Students converged at the Amphitheatre, on campus, in support of their desired prospective president. This was a determining night, a night in which flag-bearers lost or gained more support. On presenting their manifestos, a question-and-answer period followed. A candidate who did not impress the spectators might lose his chance of winning the elections, even if he was on top during the campaign before that night. The candidates had dedicated supporters who belonged to camps, but the election results were also influenced by registered floating voters. The manifesto night was also a night of interaction by supporters of the same camp, planning how to utilize their franchise.

On the day of the elections, voters of the same camp assembled, getting ready for balloting. This activity was mostly manned by a well-armed team of the Sierra Leone Police Force, especially if the campaign process was very violent. The elections normally began at about 09:00 hours and continued up to about 17:00 hours, the same day. Voters cast two forms of ballots: one for the presidency, and another for representatives of the Student Ruling Council - SRC. The completion of the voting process was followed by an immediate count in the presence of everyone, which depicted real transparency. There might have been irregularities, as in other elections around the world, but I don't believe it ever influenced a change in victory. The presidential candidate who emerged as the winner was announced instantly. This was always succeeded by great jubilation, and celebrations, by fans of the winner – Bubu-dances and other forms of making their president proud. In some cases, you could see students who portrayed themselves as members of a particular camp, celebrating the victory of another camp – watermelon politics. That was very much captivating: a true irony. But all that made campus elections too funny and sweet. After the release of election results, the safety of campus was precarious until after approximately two weeks, as winning supporters ridiculed losing opponents - an event often followed by confrontations, fights, and the throwing of missiles against opposing camps. A student was stabbed during one of the fights, which led to the intervention of the University Authorities and the Police Force, followed by disciplinary action. The disciplinary committee investigated and students who fell short gained the required penalties, based on the laws and regulations of the University, coupled with the constitutional laws of Sierra Leone, as that was a state offence.

One of the most interesting elections in my day was that involving the presidential contest between Imran Sillah and Peter Komeh. Peter Komeh was an Engineering Student and Imran an Arts Student. Imran represented the Black Camp whilst Peter Komeh represented the White Camp. Truly, Peter Komeh was on top of Imran during the campaign period, and gained so much support from students, for he was a very good public speaker. But the manifesto night was tough, as students from different camps, and those considered neutral were all present. And ironically, from my own perspective, Imran proved a better speaker than Peter Komeh on the Night of Manifesto, which almost genuinely twisted the outcome of the presidential election results. But Peter Komeh made himself so popular during campaign sessions that Imran's immense improvement was insufficient to make a win. Peter Komeh won the presidential election and was declared president of Fourah Bay College Student Union.

In final year, all graduating students completed projects in the form of dissertations, in partial fulfilment for the award of a Bachelor's. In our department, some students were allocated design projects that required physical implementation, and some literature-like projects. 'Lucky' students carried out design projects that had been executed in the past by former students. For some colleagues, it was just a matter of modification. I was the first student to carry out my design in our University. It was to design a 'Token Prepaid Meter System for Domestic Electricity Supply'. That project was not even among the set of projects posted for selection, and so was not an option. It was allocated to me after assigning projects to my classmates - even my preferred choices were given to other mates. Why? I couldn't understand! In the second semester, I started fighting with that design, running up and down Freetown, spending hours on the Internet on a daily basis. There were different Token Media, but I was interested in the Smart Card Type. Another alternative was the Plastic Key. But these two were very expensive, and my University wasn't ready to fund any of those projects. So my supervisor advised I use the Coin Type. I did further research, but couldn't find a Coin Design. I tried to design a system that didn't work, even in principle. Later, I decided to put it on hold because I had to go through another academic year to complete my modules.

∎∎∎

CHAPTER VI

The Revelation

Running through another final academic year, at the same level, was a demeaning experience. I was supposed to write two electrical modules, but registered Signal Analysis, Control Systems I and Power Engineering III. To most students, Signal Analysis was the most difficult electrical and electronics module we offered, as it was highly mathematical. Yes, it seemed difficult, but with hard work, you would remain comfortable. I had a pass grade in it and there was no need for a retake, but registered to make my grade better, as I had only two modules to do in a whole semester.

Lectures began, and we were in and out of class as usual. But this time, I decided to be more focused on my three modules. I avoided the popular 'Stone', and only made snap visits to maintain my affiliation with the membership of Quimanora and Deflosacs. My friends and club-mates were concerned about the change. They interpreted it negatively, but I had discussions with them, and got them to a point of understanding. I did attend some of our social activities, but permitted nothing to divert me from my focal point, making good grades in the three modules, and hence I allocated limited time to recreation. The first semester examinations were ready. Students occupied the Student Union building, Strasser-King building, the Engineering Department lecture hall and other College locations, as stated on the posted timetable. We took the exams and were awaiting results.

In our department, and I believe in other departments and faculties, the lecturing authorities sometimes revealed grades to students before they were published on noticeboards, especially at senior levels. In some cases, they did that because results processing was delayed and students had to register for a new semester. It was at the beginning of the second semester and our then-head-of-department, Dr. Minkailu Bah, started the unveiling process. It was my turn and I walked into his office in expectation. Control Systems I – I passed. Signal Analysis – I improved. Power Engineering III – another F! How? I couldn't understand. To me, and

Samuel F. Koroma

I believe to most students, Power Engineering III was one of the easiest final-year modules. I gave it the required attention. I did not underestimate it, especially taking it for the second time, but why another F? I couldn't believe it! I protested to my Head of Department, who referred me to the lecturer in charge of that module for verification. I met with that lecturer, the late Mr. Kebbie, and demanded my marked answer script, but he couldn't produce it and informed me I truly failed the module of Power Engineering III. Why? I couldn't comprehend. Mr. Kebbie responded, 'Engineering Students who are really strong in Mathematics always do well in the Electrical Department, but I don't know why you are having problems'. I couldn't explain. My Mathematics grades were very good, most of which were As and Bs, and I always demonstrated good mathematical skills in solving problems. So I couldn't explain that. I was broken-hearted. I couldn't talk to my colleagues. I couldn't speak to any of my friends and just rushed straight home. On arrival, I crawled into my bedroom, locked myself up and lay on the bed. 'How am I going to explain this to my parents?' I asked myself. 'How could I spend a third year in final year? How would I convince them I would make it for the third time? What guarantee would they hold on to? And if I quit, consider the time I'd wasted, the financial resources. How would I compensate for that?' I started thinking about travelling overseas, but what could I show for the wasted years? Some friends who were not even up to my standard had graduated, others graduating. What would be their perception about me? These thoughts continued, and soliloquy became my roommate. I decided to be a man and was prepared to fight with whatever life had to offer. I informed Kadi, who was my major sponsor. She later informed my parents. But Kadi understood academic difficulties and, instead of being furious, she encouraged me to face the challenge and not to give up on my dream: to get an Engineering Degree and become a practising Engineer. She advised me to compare the years spent and the year left. That was a true inspiration. Her husband, Solomon Gembeh, knew about the trouble, to my ignorance, as he constantly monitored my academic performance at Fourah Bay College. He is an alumnus of that great institution. My parents did not react negatively to me, but only despaired, thinking that their dream for me to become a Bachelor graduate, an Engineer, was being mired down. They consoled me and I registered for Control Systems II and Power Engineering IV. That semester, I was very unhappy. No time for 'Stone'! No time for social activities! I tried maintaining inner peace and concentrated on my modules. About two weeks before the second semester examinations, I left home to reside on campus, to help avoid being distracted. My departure to campus was accompanied by my then-girlfriend, Janice, and her friend, Mariama Kakay. On arrival, Janice drove past the Wisdom Tree, which was located at the diverging points of the Bai Bureh, Solomon Caulker and Davidson Nicol hostels. A comfortable sitting structure was planted around the Wisdom Tree, which made it an ideal student gossip laboratory. By the time a visitor or someone of interest approached and was going through that point, an oral surgical operation could have been completed already. Most times, students sat around that shaded location, especially in the evening, discussing different issues. It was a real 'kongosa' point, 'kongosa' meaning 'gossip' in my local Krio dialect. Janice and Mariama dropped me off and headed back home. I was a member of the Davidson Nicol Hall, but had no accommodation, so I squatted with two of my classmates who happened to be my then-Squadis in Quimanora, Sow and Jalloh - we were three in the room. I was a 'gorilla', as that was the nickname for a squatting personality.

One afternoon, I was on the table, doing some mathematical analysis, related to one of my electrical modules, when I heard a sound: it was my cell phone. I didn't look at the number. I just picked up and heard a familiar male voice: my father. 'Hello, Papa', I said, as that was how we normally referred to him. He didn't say much, just instructed me to be home urgently. Why? I couldn't figure it out. Normally, if Papa wanted to give me anything, he would send his driver or anybody available at home, and would explain to me on the phone. But that time he sounded different! I closed my book, dropped my pen, got dressed and headed downtown. I went straight into Papa's bedroom. He was seated right on his bed, with Mum standing by him, and asked me to shut the door.

I took a seat with a careful and non-distracted mind. With a quavering voice, Papa started, 'Samou, I want you to be a man, OK? Be strong, no negative reaction, OK?' That was strange! I had no clue what Papa was about to say. I replied, 'yes, sir', and suddenly something dropped within me. I thought something awful had happened to Kadi, as she was my main sponsor. But, again, I thought my Mum and Dad could've been more depressed, and their reaction could've been different. That got me further confused. I was really attentive and Papa continued, 'your stepmother and her sister made a true confession, under the conviction of a witch doctor, that she and her sister performed witchcraft rituals for you not to ever graduate from the University, nor to ever travel overseas, and even if you go in search of a job, you would never find one. And they further said that, whenever they came from their witchcraft operations, they wiped their hands on you as they entered the house. Your Mum and I didn't want to tell you; we wanted to conceal it and handle it our way, but your baby sisters, Alimatu and Abibatu, have been distressing me to let you know before things get out of hand, as they couldn't figure out the troubles you're facing at the University. They know you're brilliant'. Dad tried to hide it because he knew how I would react to situations of that nature. But in that case, instead of being violent, I wept. Of more than thirty biological children, I was not among the first twenty, but the first to succeed in Secondary School Sciences, and the first to enter University for a Bachelor's. At some point, I thought I was stupid, I thought I was lazy, I thought I was misplaced, until it was revealed that my intense academic struggle at Fourah Bay College was due to witchcraft manipulation. Travelling overseas for greener pastures, ignoring academic pursuit, was a tradition in my family. So opting for a University Bachelor's invited demonic intrusion. I was fighting to mount up the name of the Koroma family on a flag pole, lifting family members, as I hustled every second of the clock. And quickly, I ran into my bedroom with tears raining down from my eyes like the falling waters of the Bumbuna hydro-electric dam in Sierra Leone. But, as I wept, I recalled a mysterious incident that befell me during my studies on campus, in preparation for the first semester examinations, when I failed Power Engineering III for the second time. After studying for a while, my colleagues and I decided to take some rest. The three of us lay in bed, with me towards the edge, by the window. In a dream, a tall, dark lady attacked me and we were engaged in a real fight. She held onto my head and I tried getting her hands off, but to no success. She then leaned me against a metal rail and, in seconds, threw me on the ground. Instantly, I woke up and found myself physically thrown on the floor, in the room. I really felt the impact! I looked at my watch, and it was about 3:00 AM. How? I couldn't tell. That was an enigma! One of my friends, the one who was very close to me, woke up and I explained my encounter, but he treated it trivially, and later, we all laughed about it. We were all 'Enjoyers' who hardly handled spiritual issues seriously. At about 07:00 hours, we got ready to leave the dormitory for Power Engineering III. In E.J. Hall, question papers were distributed. I read through and everything was familiar, and I expected nothing worse than an 'A', but I could remember something that happened. As soon as I started the examination, I made lots of mistakes until approximately thirty minutes before the end. Truly, I ignored those mistakes and thought I would make at least the minimum pass grade. And really, one of my colleagues informed me that according to Mr. Kebbie, some students failed due to simple mistakes, and I knew I was not an exception. Mr. Kebbie did not tolerate scratches. Physically, I believe that was how I failed Power Engineering III, though both of my colleagues passed. I explained the dream to my Mum and she advised me to get back to Ghana and continue my Engineering course. Like Dad, my Mum was a Muslim and so had no good Christian foundation. I was involved in social activities, but was spiritually inclined to some extent, and knew that travelling would not help because there is no distance in the spirit.

As I thought about what to do, that revelation reminded me of Jamiru. He was very brilliant in school. When I completed my Ordinary Level course at the Prince of Wales School, my brother had just completed his third form. Remember he was the best pupil at that level. But when he started his fourth form, he got totally distracted from his coursework. Jamiru began dodging classes; he would go to 'Papsam', a popular ghetto that was around St. Edward's Secondary School in Freetown, and got into lots of destructive extracurricular activities, together with some friends. He engaged in doping practices, intoxicating himself with all sorts of drugs. He could no longer concentrate on his academia. He used his school fees and cash for lunch to purchase harmful drugs, just to satiate his passion. Any amount of money given to him he would use to buy those drugs, and ended up achieving nothing at his final examinations. Eventually he dropped out of school. Our parents then stopped offering him money to preclude him from destroying himself. They advised all family members to stop giving him money. But he sometimes got cash from his close friends who were also in the same business. In deficit situations, he stole items at home to trade in exchange of money just to get his stuff – it appeared as an addiction. When we realized and closely monitored him, he had no chance to plunder from home. So he started running outside, searching for cash and items to steal elsewhere. In some instances, he got physically beaten helpless, and we would run to his rescue. That practice continued and we got frustrated with his attitude. Papa locked him up a number of times at the police station, to enable him keep a steady head, but returned to his negative acts when released. At some point, he picked up a knife, attempting to stab even his own mother – our mother. Our parents almost gave up and decided to confine him at the City of Rest, a place setup for wayward children, headed by Pastor Ngobeh. He was shackled for about six months. This was to purge his system of any intoxicating drug-related substance, and get him ready for reintegration into society. At City of Rest, they counselled them, taught them Biblical principles and fed them squarely. They were well taken care of. My parents paid him constant visits and realized he was fit to get back into the family. For a while, he was alright. He behaved as the normal Jamiru. But after some time, he resumed his abnormal operations. Our parents got truly agitated and finally disowned him. My brother wandered the streets of Freetown – roaming aimlessly. Later, he came back to his senses after wasting years without an acceptable educational certificate. You could see that the plan was not to send him to the grave, but to destroy his academic ambition. A brilliant pupil with a dream and the potential to become an outstanding lawyer could not even qualify to become an ordinary court clerk – his fantasy was smashed. As I recalled my brother's incident, proposed Spiritual solutions started running through me. I attended some church meetings where I fed on true Biblical teachings, but I wasn't really committed. I was just a 'church-goer'. But immediately I ran to meet my Pastor, Apostle Akintayo Sam-Jolly, now Bishop, General Overseer of the Living Word of Faith Outreach Ministries International. He was unavailable. He travelled, but fortunately his assistant Rev. Joshua Alpha, to whom I submitted an oral summary of the 'Revelation', was at the Faith Cathedral. He laid on his hands and prayed for me, and requested my return for total deliverance after the second semester examinations. I returned to campus and continued preparation for the examinations.

As a student, I was also running a clothing business on Kadi's behalf. She shipped female and some male items from Texas during Christmas and Easter holidays which I distributed to female student friends, mostly on campus, especially members of the Deflosacs, Dahlia and Syramax, and the male items to some members of Quimanora and other friends. I issued some on campus and some picked up theirs at home because I had no official shop. Distribution didn't take much of my time, as I used my relaxing time on campus, and some leisure time at home, an activity that didn't last for more than three weeks. I released them on credit for about a month, though sometimes some paid on receiving and others via deposits. So, as a student, I was most times in possession of good cash, which included foreign currencies. I went to campus with my suitcase which couldn't open without the required code, and that code was only known by me. In addition to other items, I had some Leones and $50, which were more than enough to support me through the examinations period. About a week to my first module, I had only thirty thousand Leones (Le 30,000) left, and decided to go and exchange the $50 downtown, because I was running out of Leones. That was approximately two hundred and fifty thousand Leones. I opened my suitcase, got into the pouch, my usual hiding place, and couldn't find the note. I carefully removed all items at a time in search of that cash, and still couldn't find it. I searched every corner of the room: nothing was found. I had just distributed items and, during that process, spent lots of cash on phone calls, notifying faithful customers. My monthly allowance from my sister was about two weeks away and I had received nothing from customers. I had about two weeks on campus, how could I cope? I couldn't continue studying without food! I said 'God, what's this?' I didn't waste time. I gave Kadi a call, informed her about my plight, and she instantly sent me $100. I was exhilarated, as if it were a thousand dollars. My exams were my focus: to complete.

I completed the examinations and went back to project work, as my supervisor, Mr. Bangura, intimated me that if I completed the project, they might offer me concession to graduate because I had only one module against me. I fought very hard and came up with a reasonable design, theoretically, which my supervisor accepted. The design was divided into two parts: the Mechanical Coin Mechanism and the Electronic Circuitry. The Coin Mechanism was made up of the Flyer, Coin Slot, Pouch/Collector. The Micro-Switch, which was part of the Electronic Circuit and was the interface between the Coin Mechanism and the Electronic Circuitry, was attached to the inner wall of the Coin Mechanism. The Electronic Circuit comprised the Micro-Switch, the D.C. power supply, the Timing Circuit, the Electromagnetic Relay and a test-lamp. With a coin inserted into the slot, it drove the Flyer upwards, which exerted force at the base of the Micro-Switch, which closed and triggered the Timer. The Timer operated the Relay and AC power supplied to the Lamp. As a prototype, the system was designed to operate for a minute. Practically, the Coin Mechanism and Electronic Circuit were built. The Coin Mechanism operated with the Micro-switch and the Timing Circuit, the components of which I got from the late Mr. Tim, for the designed period – 60 seconds. But configuring the whole system to produce the required output became an obstacle. Time was running out, and I decided to do my write-up, putting the laboratory work on hold. In the previous year, I had started word-processing the project work, which was saved on my cousin's desktop, in his office. When I approached Sheku Fobay, he replied that his hard drive had a crash and my entire literature had been deleted and could not be recovered. I couldn't understand what was going on! Working on a write-up for months, and all I could find was an empty hard drive. I trusted my cousin, but was confounded, and started thinking about how to re-do my work, to get it ready for my supervisor's approval. Fortunately, I was still in possession of the hand-written manuscript. Typing was difficult, but I made up my mind to maintain a good sense of pertinacity. My write-up was completed, and when I presented it to my supervisor, it was rejected. He replied, 'if your system doesn't produce the desired results, I'm not going to have a look at your write-up'. It was about a week before his travel to London, which was a usual practice. I replied, 'Sir, you would be travelling in a week, so I decided to do my write-up for you to edit and sign before your departure. I'll be struggling with the practical work and I promise it would work before the Viva-Voc, which was about three months away. But, if I concentrate on the practicals, ignoring the write-up, there's no way you would edit and sign, because you would not be around'. He said, 'Okay; let me take a look at your laboratory work first.' He viewed my work and responded, 'you're using 12V supply, why are you using 555 Timer which uses 5V?' I replied, 'sir, the 555 Timer I employ uses a range of (3-15) V, so 12V falls within'. He was mute, because he knew I was right. He continued 'well, then go ahead and let your system operate'. All stages of my design operated independently, and the outputs of preceding stages were enough to drive succeeding stages, but configuring it to produce the final signal output was a real big fight. I tried troubleshooting, but couldn't detect the fault. He was my supervisor, but offered me no helping hand. Again, he rejected my write-up and vowed that as long as he remained a Lecturer in that Department, I would never get a Bachelor's, as far as Fourah Bay College was concerned, and that he would not supervise me any more.

    I got infuriated and immediately adopted a reckless attitude. I was nonchalant and you could see intense frustration. I didn't care about the consequences! I had given up and was prepared to abandon the course. We engaged in an intellectual fight in which he was unable to defeat me. It was only one of my close friends, Abubakarr Sow, who succeeded in calming me down. Yes, the project was causing me trouble, but was upset, not because of the project, but because of his vow. That man was my supervisor, but technically he offered me no help. Other supervisors technically supported their mentees, and accepted write-ups from some of my mates, even though their laboratory work was not complete. As long as they saw progress, they inspired them to move forward. I was struggling on my design with no assistance from him, and all he could do was rebuke me. Just after our oral fight, I was still in the laboratory, together with some of my classmates who had almost completed their project work. They walked up to where I was working, and wanted to give me a helping hand. They wanted all of us to work as a team on that project, but when they actually knew what I was working on, they realized my design was an electromechanical giant and left me alone. My supervisor travelled, and that was how we got separated.

It was after the quarrel that I came to my senses, remembering the 'Revelation' and said, 'Oh, the Revelation has been fulfilled; I would never graduate. No matter what, how could I talk to my supervisor, a key lecturer in my department, in that mood?' It appeared as if I was out of my senses. After that fight I was back home, but this time with a determination to quit my course and travel back to Ghana. Kadi exhorted me to hold on. She travelled to Freetown, trying to work out some documentation to take me along to the United States, but it didn't work out, and she travelled back. I stayed home, swimming in a pool of perplexity. Again, Kadi advised me to continue the academic fight. She emphasized I must get that Bachelor's degree from that institution. 'But how about my supervisor?' I thought. Kadi coaxed me and I was ready to pursue that Engineering qualification more than ever. Reader, it was on my return to home that I received the full account of the 'Revelation'. People were hesitant to tell me, but when they knew my father had started already, they uncovered the hidden package.

My stepmother and her sister made the true confession after being arrested and convicted by a witch-doctor, in the early hours of the morning. She was later conveyed to a pastor, in Wellington, the east end of Freetown, and under the anointing made the utterance Papa reported. The Servant of God and team paid a home visit for special prayers, and in the Spirit, one of the sisters in the Congregation revealed that a dark lady was moving a black folder out of my bedroom. She never knew my bedroom. She never knew I had a black folder, but gave the right description and pointed to the door of my bedroom. Do you see how the Holy Spirit works? I had two files – a black and a blue – but I used the black one often, to take to lectures, as it went with all colours and recognizing its dusty state was very hard. A witch-doctor was in my neighbourhood and, as soon as he saw me, he enquired from someone whose son I was. The person replied, 'Nyangbe'. And he continued, 'Oh! They've tampered with his education'. Those were his exact, interpreted words. So you can see the continuity in the whole process. According to them, all those 'Revelations' came up in about a week, as the event was ongoing. I even witnessed a scene in which my stepmother's sister was confessing, whilst my stepmother was in captivity.

The day after the quarrel, I forwarded a letter of complaint to the Head of Department, explaining my supervisor's decline to oversee me. My then Head of Department, Professor Redwood-Sawyerr, was very busy, so he minuted the letter and referred me to the Acting Head of Department, Dr. Minkailu Bah. As soon as I stepped into his office, he informed me that my supervisor had complained already. I tried to explain, but he did not allow me. The Head of Department revealed that my supervisor mentioned I disrespected him, calling him a fool, and that he knew nothing about my project. Yes, we had an oral fight and words were uttered, but I couldn't remember unleashing anything of that sort. I also presented my write-up to the Acting Head of Department, who refused it on the premise that he would not accept a project he didn't supervise. He was right! I went back to my supervisor in a contrite tone, but he insisted 'no' and walked me out of his office. I did everything in my capacity to reconcile with him, but he remained repulsive.

Two years in final year - no graduation!

■■■

CHAPTER VII

My Final Year in Final Year

Frustration was underway as I wrestled to register for a third year in final year. My first day on campus was like walking in a vacuum, as all of my old classmates had graduated, except for a few who dropped out due to various reasons. I picked up a course form and began the usual registration process - finance, library, and getting the Head of Department's signature. I submitted my form to the secretary, but guess what? The new Head of Department, Dr. Joseph Kanu, had travelled, and the acting Head of Department was my 'friend', my former supervisor. My course form was submitted to him, which he rejected. He didn't sign. 'Sir, why didn't you sign my form?' I asked. He replied, 'just wait, you'll soon receive a letter that is due to you'. 'Which letter?' I responded. He was off his seat, hurrying straight into the Dean's office, trying to bring up conditions for me to be expelled from the University. Later, I arrived at the Dean's and tried to verify, but he unveiled nothing about the acting Head of Department's visit. I enquired from the Dean's secretary, who confirmed his visit to the Dean's office, but disclosed nothing about their discussion. I viewed a document in preparation on the secretary's desk, but it wasn't clear as she didn't want me to decipher the content. I enquired from the Head of Department's secretary, but she was unaware of the whole game. About two weeks later, the document finally arrived at the Head of Department's secretary's desk, with conditions that my 'supervisor' thought would prevent me from registering for that school year. During that process, however, the new Head of Department returned from Ghana. My course form was submitted directly to him, and he signed it immediately. I completed my registration process and lectures began for the first semester's assessment. Again, I tried reconciling with my 'supervisor', but he remained uncompromising. The issue I reported to Dr. Joseph Kanu, who then became my new supervisor for that project. The former Head of Department, Dr. Bah, was a close friend of my former supervisor. Whatever Mr. Bangura relayed to him, regarding my issue, he accepted as final without considering my own input. But he was appointed Minister of Education of the Sierra Leone Government, and was then focused on his political career. So he had no time for our departmental struggle. He was then replaced by Dr. Joseph Kanu, who truly understood what was transpiring between Mr. Bangura and I, and addressed it without bias.

It was time for the first semester examinations and I moved to campus as usual. This time, I was in a room with one of my classmates called Mojo. He was new in final year and my then Junior Quimanora-mate also. Approximately four days before my Power Engineering III examination, I had another dream of the same lady in the 'Revelation', fighting with me. She bit the back of my right palm, the hand I use to write, and held on to it. I tried retracting my hand from her mouth, but could not. Again, I was inspired from within to shout the Name of Jesus. And as soon as I shouted 'Jesus', she left my hand and fled. The Almighty God revealed her true identity, but I did not make any physical confrontation. I knew it was a spiritual battle. At that time, I was leading a prayerful life. I was focused on Jesus, so she did not succeed. But, in two days, I got a very high fever. I was sick. I couldn't study effectively, but thank God who directed me to study hard before that demonic attack. For two days I couldn't read. I didn't inform my parents, to avoid taking heavy medication, and I knew the problem was spiritual. I went into the examination hall sick, but was able to complete four questions out of five. We vacated, and soon it was time for project work again.

I took up my design work again during the first semester break. As I walked into the skeletal electrical laboratory, most of my components could not be located. I reported this to the laboratory technician, but his response was deplorable - he could not account for the missing electronic components. Even with the cheapest alternative, the Coin Design, my department could not provide the materials I needed. I had to personally buy parts and worked from what was available. So the loss of those components promoted my frustration. I had to strive around town to purchase them again. When I wanted to practically build my coin mechanism, I went to the Mechanical Engineering department, but there was no headway and I had to run down to the Congo Cross campus of the Milton Margai College of Education and Technology, in search of a more advanced workshop, and was able to do my mechanical implementation with the aid of Mr. Volima — who was a lecturer at Fourah Bay College and The Milton Margai College of Education and Technology. The troubles I encountered were explained to my new supervisor, who later requested a demonstration of my design. I set up the prototype, demonstrated it, and he knew I had been working hard, even though the system did not operate as expected. He requested my write-up, which I speedily handed over to him.

We resumed the second semester and it was time for the first semester results to be published. 'Gosh...' I thought, as dread enveloped my nurtured confidence. The staircase to my Engineering Bachelor's began to jiggle. That was a module I had failed twice and the result of my third attempt was about to be released. You could imagine my state. That was my last chance! Failing that module implied expulsion. I would be diplomatically advised by University officials to readily withdraw from the course. The results were posted and I was about forty metres from the noticeboard. I walked closer and shut my eyes as I snailed towards it, maintaining my concentration. My hands were stretched forwards, and suddenly I felt a hard substance; it was the noticeboard. Cautiously, I opened my eyes with increasing heartbeat rate and carefully located the final-year category, running through our registration numbers. I was not too far from the start, as I was a very senior student in that class, having been doing it for three years. I located the single module against that number, and for the first time, I enjoyed genuine joy, total peace and true happiness in my academic scrimmage. Finally, I got a hard-earned 'B' in Power Engineering III. Immediately, I gave Kadi a call, called my father, my mother, informing them about my true academic success. I ran home in exhilaration, as I viewed my younger siblings jubilating. They were really happy - they knew I finally made it.

Not too long after publication of results, finalists were invited to verify their records at the examinations office. I looked through my proposed transcript and detected some errors. Some module grades were missing, of which two were departmental – a final year's and a second year's. The other grades from other departments were quickly resolved. I got in contact with my former supervisor again, because he was responsible for preparing results. He was very strategic in our department. I informed him about my two missing grades, and he promised to remit them to the examinations office as soon as possible. Later, he informed me he found one, but couldn't find the other. According to him, he couldn't find the second year grade. Why? He didn't explain. About a week later, I went to the examinations office to confirm receipt of my grades. The two non-departmental grades were in, but my electrical modules were still hanging. One of the departmental grades was Engineers-in-Society – EIS – in which I got an A. It was a final-year grade, so that would've been easy for me to trace, but for the second-year module, it would have been difficult. Immediately, I registered the missing second-year Applied Electricity II module for the second semester examination to counter any opposing action, as I wanted nothing to preclude my graduation. Reader, my final-year module was submitted, but the second-year grade was not released. Applied Electricity II was one of the criteria to enter the Electrical Department, in third year, so there was no doubt it was part of my result. But where did it go? I couldn't perceive it. The loss of my grade was confirmed about four days to the start of the second-semester examinations. I rushed around students of that level, seeking notes, as I was not in possession of those educational materials anymore. I was blessed to find a friend, Amad, who released his notes to me for duplication. Ahmad was also my junior club-mate: an Enjoyer. I photocopied the notes and returned them in a few hours. Since that module was a junior electrical course, I knew I wouldn't have much difficulty in understanding. So I stayed home and hibernated. I ran through the notes and was ready to face the examination. Just before we started that exam, I prayed. The results were published, and I passed with a 'B' in Applied Electricity II, truly marking the end of my written intellectual confrontation at Fourah Bay College.

At the end of the academic year, I got sick but treated it trivially. I didn't go to the hospital, and ingested a few minor tablets. A few days later, my condition improved and I was fine. After about two weeks, I fell ill again, but this time with a strange feeling from within. I then decided to consult a medical doctor, who recommended laboratory tests. The results were out and I was diagnosed with typhoid fever and acute malaria. Typhoid fever is caused by the bacterium 'bacillus salmonella' which lives in and combats your digestive system. There're two types - 'O' and 'H'. Many people get infected with either the 'O' or 'H', but I was infected with both. The doctor made a prescription, and I started going through his medication. In few days, my situation exacerbated. I couldn't believe it! A qualified medical doctor put me on the right medication, and the drugs I bought from the Chinese hospital were no counterfeits. This, I reported to the doctor and he referred me to the dispensary for drug verification. The drugs were verified, they were no fake! They even went to the extreme and gave me similar drugs of a different manufacturer. I went home, and at about 13:00 hours, I started shivering seriously and my father sent for a renowned qualified nurse in our neighbourhood, Aunty Aisha, who administered me some drugs in the form of drips. Later, I experienced some side-effects like dimmed vision and dizziness. The next day, I was fine. I had lost considerable amounts of weight and started taking some vitamin tablets to help restore my lost physical stature. In few days, I started regurgitating everything I took in, both solid food and liquid. I got sick sometimes, but that was incredible. I've never been ill that way. I rushed to the hospital, this time without even informing my parents. I had tests and all the doctor could see was indigestion. He prescribed drugs which I didn't bother to buy, let alone take, as I was confused. I ran to another nurse, who insisted on giving me an injection. I took it and went back home, but still wasn't fine. Later, when I got into my bedroom, I vowed not to take any of the drugs again. I opened an oral rehydration salt sachet and dissolved it in a litre of water. In my exact words I said, 'Heavenly Father, let this solution represent the Blood of Jesus, as I drink from it, let the healing power of the Blood of Jesus flow through me and let me be made whole'. I drank the solution and was instantly healed; no more drugs, no more vomiting. Jesus healed me!

When Moinya was about to write her Ordinary-Level examinations, she got tied in an incomprehensible situation. She could feel a physical substance, like a ball, moving through her oesophagus – up and down. Initially, she thought she had swallowed something irritating. She tried every method to get it out, but there was nothing she could do. Papa took her to a medical doctor and other medical personnel, but all efforts yielded no good output. Moinya was devastated; she was in continued trauma, thinking of her medical predicament. Our parents did all they could, but to no avail. She was distracted from her coursework. Moinya was intelligent, especially in English Language. She only got delivered when she had an encounter with our Lord Jesus, through a man of God, after wasting time without attaining a good height in education. During a deliverance session, she vomited demonic substances in the physical realm. You could see that the idea was not to send her to eternity, but to obstruct her academic pursuit. Since that time, Moinya was born again, left home for Ghana, and later travelled to the United Kingdom. Her situation, and that of Jamiru, were about to make a duplication in my life. But I refused to give up the fight. I pursued my academic destiny, right in my father's house, and was ready for any Spiritual fight, because I knew there is no distance in the Spirit and Jesus is the only Answer.

I continued fighting, and during that terrible illness, I received a call from my friend, Khai, to carry out a contract. We were very close at the University and also in the same neighbourhood. From my response, she knew I was sick and advised me to get back to her as soon as I was okay, which I did. Then, she informed me about 'The Teacher Verification' project, using special software, and would like to work with me. She also asked me to help recruit about twenty people, mostly students, to work with us, which I did. Amongst which were Abraham Maada Tucker, Two-three, Ramou, Old-skool, and others, most of which were students of Fourah Bay College. We were trained and everything was set; then we started the two-week project. At our centre, I worked with a close friend of mine, Kainde, who was also a Deflo-member, at Rokel Secondary School Structure. The contract was awarded by the Ministry of Education to register teachers countrywide using a biometric system. The main objective was to eliminate 'Ghost Teachers'. It was during the long vacation in August. The system comprised a fingerprint scanner, a digital camera, a laptop computer on which the biometric software was installed, powered by a 230V alternating current generator. I won't specify other generating parameters. We started work at approximately 07:00 hours. In verifying a teacher, you input his personal details, scanned all ten fingers, and took snap shots of his documents, which were saved on the software. But initially, my fingerprint scanner could not operate. I performed different tests — wiped it dry with a clean cloth, wiped my finger dry, disconnected and reconnected the connector, and all required tests yielded no positive result. This I reported to one of the supervisors, but he thought it was something else. Together with Khai, he rushed to our centre. Khai tested the fingerprint scanner and realized it was truly faulty. She had to replace it, and I continued my job. Teachers from different institutions queued up as their verification process continued. I can remember the late Mr. Kawa of Albert Academy Secondary School was verified at our Centre. At some point, I realized some were without their educational certifications and other essential personal documentation. So I had to address them, informing them that whosoever was without any required document could not be verified as a teacher. The affected then rushed to get their documents, as me and Kainde continued verifying.

The 20th August was the date set for our viva, and my write-up was still with my supervisor. The deadline for submission was almost there. During lunch break, I went to my Head of Department's office, but he didn't show up on that day. When I arrived at his isolated residence, with a pacified atmosphere, there were dogs lying around, but I headed straight to the door. They seemed tired, at a shaded location. Then, I hit the front door with a knock and heard a familiar voice say, 'there's someone at the door'. A girl, whose face was almost identical to that of my Head of Department, opened the door. My right foot initiated the first step into his home, followed by my not-very-energetic left. As I approached the living room, somebody was seated on a reddish relaxing chair. I saluted, 'Good afternoon sir!' He replied, 'How are you, Koroma?' 'Fine, Sir', I responded. We discussed my dissertation, and he promised to let me have the edited version on the next day. I exited and was back to work. The day rolled by and the next morning met me at my Head of Department's office. Something strange happened! My supervisor couldn't remember being in possession of my write-up. He asked me to make a search for the folder containing my dissertation. I looked through every corner of his desk, and right beneath other files, I found my un-edited write-up. What? That was the deadline! He apologized and asked me to see him in three days. I left, with exasperation, and was back to work. On the day of our appointment, I arrived at his office, but he was nowhere to be found. Again, I met him at his residence and again we made another appointment. I arrived at his office, at about midday, and to my greatest astonishment he could not be located. I gave him a call and he replied he left the office about thirty minutes before my arrival, but left my edited write-up with his office runner, Ansu. I received it and went straight to the computer room downtown. I couldn't complete the relevant corrections without going there, and had to go there again, temporarily abandoning my job. As I continued correcting, numerous calls hit my phone because my absence at work created some troubles. We were only two at the centre and I was the head. I was practically supervising our centre. But my dissertation or that job – which was supposed to be the forgone alternative? I left and promised to be at work soon. I completed my editing and went straight up to campus for binding. There were lots of dissertations to be bound, but I paid the guy extra cash as a matter of urgency. We made an agreement to pick up our packages at about 16:00 hours, but he assured me he'd be there until 18:30 hours and I went back to work. The pressure kept me working, and I was able to be on campus at about 17:30 hours. Guess what? The library was closed. That was an hour before his agreed departure time. Gosh! I couldn't submit on the final deadline. I tried calling my supervisor, but couldn't get him on the phone. It was Friday and I had to wait another weekend. I went home again, disappointed. On the following Monday morning, I went straight to the library, picked up my three bound copies of dissertation, and headed to the department. Dr. Joseph Kanu was not in his office. I then spoke with his secretary, but said nothing of substance about his coming. Instantly, I picked up a cab and moved towards his residence. On my way, I spotted him in an opposing moving car. I then returned and intercepted him at Model Junction. I troubled him. He couldn't listen to me. He got agitated. But I insisted, and he finally gave me audience. Dr. Kanu instructed me to drop the copies at his secretary's, which I speedily did. Afterwards, I rushed back to work, at about midday, and finally concluded the job about two hours later. I rested on Tuesday and Wednesday, and in my quiet time, I just heard a voice from within, reminding me about my dissertation. There were three blank sections provided in it, just after the title cover - one for my supervisor's signature, one for mine and the third for date of submission. The voice re-echoed that I didn't sign my space provided. At once, I called my supervisor, who promised to be in his office in three hours. He requested another demonstration of my practical work, which I did, and he signed his part. He then invited me into his office, asking why I did not sign. I explained that it was because of the hurry. He accepted this, and asked me to sign all three copies of my dissertation. He dated all copies and asked me to hand two of them to the secretary.

Reader, my dissertation was truly submitted on 13th August, 2008.

The viva was set for 20th August, 2008. But guess what? My name did not appear on the noticeboard. Why? I couldn't figure it out. I enquired, and realized the list of prospective graduates and their corresponding external examiners was posted by my former supervisor. It wasn't a surprise! My name was omitted, and he had travelled to London. I ran to my Head of Department, in protest of that 'uprise'. He explained there was no justification for not publishing my name. Then, he transmitted a message to the secretary, instructing her to post my name on the noticeboard.

The viva vocal arrived - 20thAugust, 2008. My external Examiner was Mr. P. Tarawallie, of whom I had never known, and it was my turn. At about 15:00 hours, the examiner walked out of his office and announced my name with a question, 'Is it Koroma?' I jumped up and moved towards the huge dark figure. He turned as I hurried after him into the very small office. He was a nice man, but sounded very strict. Initially, he posed personal questions. We had some friendly conversation and he tactically got into the dissertation proper. In our discourse, he asked both Mathematical and Literature questions, and I believe he was impressed by my response. At a point, he requested to take a look at the hardware of my design. I took the lead and was later joined by Mr. Tarawallie. I set up the system and started the demonstrating process. The Coin was inserted, which drove the Flyer and activated the Micro-Switch. The Micro-Switch triggered the Timing Circuit, but the Electromagnetic Relay did not operate and so the Lamp could not illuminate. There could've been a loose connection between the Timing Circuit and Relay. The Relay Coil could have been open. There were many other probable causes. I tried troubleshooting, but Mr. Tarawallie put me on hold, as time was limited. So he asked lots of questions on the design and I was able to put up a very good technical defence about my presentation. He invited me again into his office for the final judgement. I was a bit disturbed, as he skimmed through his appraisal. Mr. P. Tarawallie made his final statement and finally said, 'you are okay'. He asked whether I had anything to say. I nodded in disagreement, but said, 'thank you, sir.' I left his office with an elated heart and joined my colleagues for refreshment in our department. I was served a plate of fried rice, together with some snacks, and an ice-cold bottle of orange drink – Fanta. My supervisor, my Head of Department, Dr. Joseph Kanu, asked about the exam, and I informed him it was okay. He smiled and replied, 'Thank you, Koroma'. I arrived home after that tough oral and practical examination, and slept for hours. I knew I put up a successful defence, but was later worried about something. At Fourah Bay College, you only confirm your progress when you see your final result, especially in my case.

During the vacation, I heard rumours from classmates that our project grades were ready. I ran straight to my Head of Department. As soon as I stepped into his office, he said, 'congratulations, Koroma'. I replied 'Thank you, sir'. He revealed my grade and I got a C+. Later, I went to the College Secretariat, checked at the Examinations Office to ensure all my grades were intact, and verified I was qualified for graduation. Just on my way out, right at the door, I was faced with my former supervisor. He was just back from London and knew I had completed all prerequisites to graduate. We stared at each other, eye to eye, for a few seconds. After that brief period of looking, he smiled, and I did the same. We crossed each other without saying a word and I rushed home in ecstasy. My name was later published, at the University Secretariat, among other graduands for the convocation ceremony, set for 13th December, 2008. I settled all my bills, got my materials ready for the ceremony... and there emerged another trouble.

■■■

CHAPTER VIII

The Graduation Ceremony

Kadi's husband, Dr. Solomon Gembeh, was supposed to travel with my graduation suit to Freetown. He couldn't get an earlier flight, so I decided to go to town, about two days before the graduation ceremony, to get my black attire. I got a nice one and was on my return in a taxi. As I travelled back, there was traffic hold-up around Syke Street, a road close to the region where I resided, and I heard a sudden heavy sound from a direction I couldn't tell. The car then vibrated seriously and all passengers jumped out of it, with very high accelerations, realizing a four-wheel drive had run into us, just at the back of where I was seated. The back of the car crumpled, but didn't penetrate within. I laughed! Then I got another cab and arrived home safely. Until the rehearsal activity on 12th December, 2008, I refused going out.

As I thought about my graduation ceremony, something ran through my mind. During one of my third-year vacations, one afternoon, I had just from town when my father invited me for a chat. He started, 'Your sister will be graduating in September from Goldsmiths University in London, and you are highly needed; get ready for the trip'. I replied, 'But Papa, my passport is expired already,' as the date for the graduation was really close. He continued, 'Apply for another at once,' which I did, and received a reply within a week. Immediately, I arrived at the consular department of the British High Commission, located along Spur Road, Freetown, for a booking, and was offered an interview date for 27th September, 2004. That seemed hilarious. How could I get a visa when the graduation ceremony was to be held on 9th September, 2004? I made several attempts to get an earlier date, but to no avail. What troubled me was that someone who had the same problem got an earlier date and attained her visa. The graduand was my elder sister, Jorbay Koroma, who entered university two years after me. Jorbay was also very supportive in my education, especially at sixth-form level, and we had a healthy relationship. So I was exultant when I received that information. I wanted to be there, to support her achievement, but couldn't make the trip. Later, she travelled to Freetown just after her graduation, and advised me to keep that date and attend the interview for a Christmas visit. Something happened I didn't understand. On the 27th, I just felt weak and couldn't attend the interview. Jorbay and Kadi admonished me to make another appointment. I did not. They couldn't understand what was going on. Reminiscing Jorbay's graduation further strengthened me, and I knew I fought a good fight, because if I had given up, it would have been considered wasted years. But I realized that getting that Engineering Degree would add another Bachelor to the Koroma family and justify my stay at the University. As this thought continued, the cocks began to crow, utensils in the kitchen started tinkling, doors began to sound, and gradually the sun's rays began to unveil themselves, signifying the beginning of a remarkable event.

The Graduation Day

Prospective graduates of the Fourah Bay College, College of Medicine and Allied Health Sciences, and the Institute of Public Administration and Management, ran to and from the University Secretariat, located at Tower Hill, Freetown, in preparation of the annual convocation ceremony, celebrating the success of the final post of graduands for the corresponding academic year. In some cases, names of graduands were omitted due to various reasons like lack of payment of fees, and other related issues, which were sometimes sorted before the graduation day. During preparation, graduating students settled their dues, purchased or hired academic gowns, mitres, and different hoods representing different faculties. On the eve of the congregation ceremony, an approximately two-hour rehearsal process, teaching prospective graduates on issues related to procession on the graduation day, was conducted. In my case, it was carried out by senior lecturers of Fourah Bay College, on campus, in which students of the different constituent colleges participated. With resolution, we were then set for the real day.

On Saturday 13th December, 2008, smart-looking graduands from all constituent colleges of the University of Sierra Leone, dressed in their black and white attires, assembled at the Fourah Bay College Amphitheatre. Ladies put on white skirt-suits underneath their black academic gowns, mitres on heads, with black shoes and hoods representing their various faculties. Gents were clothed in black trouser-suits, with dull/non-flashy ties underneath black academic gowns, mitres on heads, black shoes and hoods representing their different faculties as well.

The procession commenced at about the top mid-point of the Amphitheatre, with the Engineering faculty in front, of which I was one of the leading students. We climbed down the steps, turned left, and assumed the sitting positions reserved for us. The congregation was full of dignitaries of the executive arm of government headed by the former president of the Republic of Sierra Leone, His Excellency Dr. Ernest Bai Koroma, together with the Minister of Education, Youths and Sports, honourable members of Parliament, University officials, lecturers from other non-governmental institutions and constituent colleges, and other distinguished personalities. The then Vice-Chancellor and Principal of the University of Sierra Leone, Professor Aiah Gbakima, was introduced, and dispensed the inception address. He addressed relevant, crucial and complicated issues which affected the university setting, especially related to student behaviour. But the most important delivery was that of the former President. Prior to the convocation ceremony, during the academic year, some students demonstrated a sense of barbarism and recklessness, which led to the suspension of social clubs on the university campuses. Former President Koroma, in his address, imposed an indefinite ban on all social clubs and strongly cautioned students and graduands to maintain a high state of discipline. He warned continuing students that if there was any recurrence of that ill-mannerism, students would not only be expelled, but face state jurisdiction. In his resolve, he conferred deserving university degrees on all graduands, as affirmed, announced by the University Vice-Chancellor.

The university convocation had always been flamboyant. Friends and families of graduands from different origins were invited. My Mum, Dad and a few relations accompanied me to that commemorating occasion. My Mum prepared delicious food, complimented by ice-cold soft drinks, which we imbibed together outside the Obelisk restaurant after receiving my Electrical and Electronics Engineering Bachelor's. We wrapped up, and I went for a cool walk at the Lumley Beach, Freetown, while my Mum, Dad, friends and other relations travelled home.

But by the time I graduated, I had broken up with Tutu, Aisha travelled to the United Kingdom, I got separated from Janice, Amie had graduated and due to my academic trouble, I lost communications with Clarissa, as all I was truly concerned about was to capture my University Bachelor's from Fourah Bay College. Clarissa and I were communicating, but through e-mails and on our landline number. Later, our landline was permanently out of service, so we were mainly communicating through electronic mails. Even though I later started using a cell phone, I didn't give Clarissa my number, for I was highly protecting that relationship – I didn't want her to know I was dating other girls, as some were also very possessive. So when I started having my university trouble, I ignored all other international communications and focused on communications related to my Engineering Course, which mostly came from Kadi. But when I was sure of my graduation, something just popped-up on my mind and I ran to an Internet Café. I sent Clarissa a message, because I knew her e-mail address by heart. But every attempt I made, replied with failed notification, implying non-existence. Prior to my University complications, Clarissa also relocated to the United Kingdom and gave me her cell phone number. But it was only written on a piece of paper. I lost it. That's how we got separated. Nevertheless, there was another personality who was an accounting student of the Njala University. Many of my friends and ex-girlfriends knew nothing about her, but she was in the dark, secretly extracting hidden tissues of my heart. We fought in my bedroom, we fought in her bedroom, we fought on the street. But even though I treated her recklessly, whenever she walked towards me, I saw a girl ever determined to fortify her matrimonial establishment. Physically, mentally, and spiritually, she struggled to put an end to illegal rivalry in my life. In spite of all my relationships, she was truly determined, constantly declaring me as her prospective husband. She knew I loved The Almighty God so much, and so her secret weapons were prayer and fasting. She prayed! She fasted for months to eliminate her illegal mates. And, as I write, she is the product of the rib that was removed from my side. So the few hours I spent at the beach, I spent with that lovely lady, Madiana Nyamu Golia, who is now Mrs. Madiana Nyamu Koroma. We walked along the seashore, ingested some soft drinks at the Family Kingdom recreational centre, located along Aberdeen Beach, and headed back home. Other family members, who did not attend the convocation ceremony due to unavailability of official invites, as we were offered only two, were awaiting my arrival to begin celebrating. Disappointedly, my decision to go to Aberdeen Beach increased their arousal and delayed their passion, but I succeeded in letting them understand it was very necessary. That was part of my cathartic process. However, they received me with open arms, jubilating in respect of my laudable achievement. We discussed relevant family matters and I started preparing for the real celebrations - the graduation party.

The Graduation Party

Traditionally, lots of new graduates host parties, celebrating their academic achievement. Some carry out their occasion on the night of the graduation day, but others chose different dates, especially close friends or graduates of the same camp or social club. I selected a date which was a week after the convocation ceremony, because the 13th of December was jam-packed with parties, to some of which I was invited. Kadi, together with her husband Solomon Gembeh, sponsored that great occasion, with some assistance from other siblings in the United Kingdom, Australia and the United States.

I started running through and across town, sorting out issues related to the party. I made estimates and arrangements for food, musical system and drinks, which included wine, and other related equipment. At about 17:00 hours, approximately two hours to the start of the party, I left in reception of the Disk Jockey and musical set. We arrived home about an hour to the beginning of that unprecedented event. The D.J. was set up, and vibration of decent classic and contemporary sounds started everything. Food was readily available and drinks locked up in my bedroom in an icy-barrel. In many African homes, family members would illegally, and cunningly, withdraw drinks from storage portions, if not properly guarded. The party began, and guests started walking in. Everybody was dressed, except me, because I ensured everything was properly set up, to avoid embarrassment. Among the guests were extended family members, fellow graduates, past graduates, continuing students, friends outside University, and friends of me and my family in the neighbourhood. The stage was set, but I was absent, taking a cool bath. My father was impatient and stepped into the bathroom, accelerating my civility. Suddenly, I rushed out of my bedroom in semi-formal attire – trousers, long-sleeved shirt and tie – and into the sitting hall. Sister Agnes Kumba Bondi, a sister of Samuel Bondi, supplied the opening prayer. Freeman was the master of ceremonies. He made the welcome address, introducing family members and other prominent personalities. On the high table were my Dad, Mum, my stepmother Isatu (Opadi), Solomon Gembeh and myself. As in normal practice, everybody expected a speech from the Celebrant, but I totally forgot about that process, because I was pre-occupied with party arrangement. After a while, 'Sir Free' (as Freeman was commonly called) asked whether I had anything to say to the assembly. I was shocked, but declining would have been a degrading response. I affirmed and picked up the microphone. Many of the guests, except for my university colleagues, recognized my potential in Mathematics, but knew little about my English Language output, especially in speeches. My family knew about my strength in Mathematics, not in English Language. But as soon as I delivered the first few phrases, the whole crowd followed with overwhelming applause. As I went deeper, the audience screamed, and I started receiving message signal tones. On conclusion, I read text messages like 'you're a real politician', and 'I never knew you were that eloquent in English Language'. Friends and members of my family hugged me, making me feel real big. I appreciated those comments, which reminded me I was very good at public speaking and an excellent reader. In school, I used to lead devotional activities, and also used to read during some literature classes, especially that taught by Mrs. Memunatu Pratt. I could remember a situation when Dr. Memunatu Pratt gave me some lashes at the Prince of Wales School. I liked a particular haircut, 'boy alinco', which she strongly advised me to cut-off. On many occasions, I promised to get rid of it, but deliberately evaded her advice as I was really in love with that hairstyle. Every time I saw her coming, I would dodge out of the class. And one day, she entered the class unannounced and instructed me to move to the front. It was during one of our literature tuitions. Mrs. Pratt took a razor blade and speedily cut off my 'boy alinco'. To me, that was horrifying! I thought my handsome looks depended on that hairstyle, and it was fashionable. Mrs. Pratt didn't show any sign of remorse and even handed me the 'Things Fall Apart' passage to read. I knew the white man was very clever, but how could fellow pupils understand that when I read with a quavering voice? However, I later realized she was working in my interests, as that earned me some amount of decency. Dr. Memunatu Pratt was one of the Mentors, if not the Chief, who helped develop my reading and speaking skills, and I salute her for that.

But even in the midst of the graduation party, my happiness was about to be distorted. Initially, I made arrangement with the D.J. to make ready a song I liked so much, 'I can be bigger...', for the opening dance. To my greatest surprise, the compact disc containing the song, which the D.J. claimed to be in possession of, could not be found. I almost got totally embarrassed. Then, I instructed the Disk Jockey to slot in an alternative as I introduced my then-honey, Madiana Nyamu Golia, on stage with a dance. The hall was in an organized chaos, screaming as I danced with my Nyamu.

Celebrations continued and it was time for dispensing food. I had no rest, running up and down, as I wanted all guests, both invited and uninvited, to remain very comfortable. A delicious meal done by female family members, supervised by my mother, was prepared at home. Many of my younger sisters including Danema, Nancy, Hannah, Alima, Moifengeh, Fatmata and Abibatu were very active during that occasion. Those young ladies energetically performed excellent waiting services, discharging both Western and African food which included pasta salad, grilled chicken, roast beef, fried rice, jollof rice, fish balls and fried shrimps, to the point of guest satisfaction. Simultaneously, my brothers, including Jamiru, Lamin, Sheku and John Foday, ensured everyone present was satisfied as far as drinks were concerned. And some guests even took away surplus, as there was an overflow of food and drinks, especially bottles of wine. Dr. Solomon Gembeh was readily seated to reinforce any shortage of drinks, when guests started flooding the party hall, but there was no need for extras, as the event was properly planned. Most of my

Quimanora friends trooped into the party house, in single file, at about 01:00 hours, who later converged outside in continuation of celebrations. They included Moi, J.J., and more. Maada Tucker, my closest Junior Quimanora friend, was always with me, and truly supported in my party arrangement. Everybody had a good time eating, drinking, dancing, and singing songs to my credit, as the photographer, Alhaji, was busy capturing images of major activities on his digital camera. The event was excellently video recorded.

Celebrations ended, as guests intermittently retired to their various homes.

■■■

CHAPTER IX

Getting Through a University

My deep undergraduate experiences, as empowered by The Almighty God, are enough to help students successfully run through a tertiary institution.

Success is an achievement. Some students commence university work without proper preparation, leading to negative consequences. There are many ways to emerge successful from a university. But outlined below are some factors which, I believe, would help you gain true academic success. And if violated, can destroy or deform your academic Destiny. They're designed for university students, but the same principles apply to other educational institutions.

Making the Right Decision

Some students ignorantly confuse themselves by making the wrong inceptive decision. Selecting a career or field of study should not be spontaneous; it has to be pre-meditated - driven by your talent and assignment. In secondary or high school, you must recognize the subjects you're good at, depending on performance, which determines and unfolds your academic flair. Many only consider their talents to determine their fields of study, ignoring their assignments. Prior to university, if you know you have an assignment to become a pastor in full-time ministry, there's no need to study to become a medical doctor. That's why some efforts are wasted, as some only get revelations of their assignments after university. They might have spent seven years or more there, and then they realize all they were created for was to be a singer. However, we're not all created to be pastors. Some are actually created to become engineers, because the buildings we sit-in during Church Services are done by civil engineers. The microphones, amplifiers, and the electricity we utilize are provided by electrical and electronics engineers. So you need to find out what you were created to do. As we get deeper, how you uncover your assignment would be unfolded.

You should have decided on your educational institution, even before high school graduation, but some people get influenced by friends. This is the point you have to handle with tremendous care. Your field of study should not be a function of the university you desire, but rather the university should be a function of your field of study. For instance, you might be a science pupil with various options. You've got Medicine, Engineering, Pure and Applied Sciences, and other science-related fields. In making your initial decision, you first consider your field of study prior to selecting the university. You might have known that your field is Medicine, but if you're crazy about Fourah Bay College, which does not offer Medicine, you may end-up in the wrong field of study, hence a deplorable career. Some students do err by desiring to attend a particular academic establishment and are only limited to the courses offered at that institution. In cases where you have different institutions offering identical courses, then you've got to go for the best.

Don't allow an institution, friend or relation to influence your course path - make the right decision. My first choice was actually Medicine, and I could've done well in it, but that was influenced by my parents. I could've done well in theory, as my Biology and Chemistry were alright, but I hated seeing blood, so that might have caused me trouble. I liked Mathematics and Physics, and was okay with the practice, so Engineering was my best option.

Getting Ready For the Interview

Admissions into tertiary institutions, especially Universities, depend, to a large extent, on your performance at the interview. Your performance at this stage helps the panel determine your true intellectual identity. You can have all 'As', but if you depict a negative academic image on interview, your intellectual capability would be questioned. Before gaining entrance into Fourah Bay College, I was invited to an interview. I had no affiliation. I was not even around. I was in Ghana and my hard copy application was dropped through Freeman. On my O-Level results, I had a '1' in General Mathematics and a '2' in English Language. If I had put up a defence that couldn't match my certification, my academic output could've been 'in the float', which might have led to rejection. But I truly defended my grades. Even after high school graduation, you continue reading until you get into the university. You can take a few days' break during vacation, but that should not steal your zeal for academia. It strengthens your academic foundation and prepares you for the interview.

After my successful Ordinary Level Examinations and during my Advanced Level Course, up to the break in Ghana, I always helped students in Mathematics without demanding a cent. That helped me remain in good shape. Even if I was to take an entrance examination at Fourah Bay College, I was prepared. Some institutions set written entrance examinations, which is another form of assessment or complement to the oral interview. But remember, in an interview, it's not all about your academic work - you must be prepared for personal and general questions, especially Intelligence Quotient tests.

In every environment, appearance is very vital. Prospective students should be in semi-formal or formal attire. Avoid wearing sexually-enticing clothing or any apparel that supports nudity. Indecency can count against you. You might not feel the effect, but when there is competition, you may greatly experience the drawback.

Try to arrive about thirty minutes before your interview, as this helps you cool down and think clearer. When you enter the interview room, do not sit until you're instructed. Salute the authorities, be upright, remain confident and get ready to face the fight.

Financial Status

On receiving acceptance into a university, one of the most important factors is your financial status. It would be almost impossible to complete your course without proper financial back-up. You need to evaluate your minimum expenditure for the academic year and make the relevant arrangements. This should include tuition and other living expenses, but recreation should only be considered when there's surplus. This evaluation is an approximation, as expenditure increases during academic sessions. For instance, lecturers could prepare handouts in your interest, which you would need to purchase. If you're sponsored, you have to be in a healthy relationship with your sponsor, and let them comprehend the need for financial increase. Many students were sponsored by governments in the form of grants. In the case of Sierra Leone, there were the Sierra Leone Grants-in-Aid – SLG – but that only covered tuition. Self-sponsored students need to ensure the necessary funds are ready or continual. A number of students have dropped out of universities due to weak cash planning or financial obstruction. They started out very well, but couldn't cope along the way. I could remember some very poor college mates who used to walk to and from campus through the popular 'canal'. 'Canal' was a hilly path leading to and from Fourah Bay College campus - it was a bypass route leading to the central or eastern part of Freetown. As the name implies, it resembled a canal. When students, most of whom couldn't afford continued transportation fare, walked through it to campus, they became fatigued, sweating profusely. How could you concentrate in the lecture room, and on your coursework, with such tiredness? Some persevered and made good grades, but others could not. Other poor students who couldn't get scholarships dropped out. Some students, supposed to become Engineers, ended up being brilliant Technicians. Some, who were wired to be doctors, ended up being nurses. You need to ensure your financial status is secured. There are cases in which students lose sponsorship due to various reasons - some due to poor academic performance; others due to the demise of sponsors. Some lose monetary support due to bad relationships with sponsors, loss of jobs, or bad businesses, in the case of the self-sponsored. In such cases, solicit an immediate source of finance, otherwise you drop out. Some students acquired the required funds for their academic pursuit, but got into superfluous expenditure. Don't be extravagant! Stop being a spendthrift! Your academic work must remain the highest priority.

Punctuality and Consistency

Punctuality and regular attendance is a great deal of a problem at the university. When students step into universities, they consider themselves bosses of their future. Many no longer listen to advice of elders, but they buy, and do, whatever they want, ignoring parental exhortation. Regular timely attendance at lectures contributes largely to your learning process. Every course begins with an introductory stage, and sometimes missing that stage makes it difficult to follow up. That leads to reduced grades, hence poorer performance. You might get the notes from other mates, but there're some statements delivered orally which could not be captured in writing. Some colleagues even misconstrue received messages. When you listen to a lecturer teach, it becomes easier to follow up his notes.

Study on a daily basis, because when you accumulate notes, you get into trouble. I knew what I went through in final year when my studies accumulated. I knew what I went through when I had incomplete notes. I had to run after colleagues to get notes, and I knew the cash I spent on photocopies to get about 90% of my notes ready. If I was broke, it could have been a disaster. That made me fatigued and further reduced my study period. Class participation is essential in continuous assessment. Some lecturers do not only consider written class tests, but attendance and participation in class as well. Try to answer questions you think you know, and don't hesitate to ask when you don't understand, or have reservation on a concept.

The Orientation Programme

Some prospective students trivialize the university orientation. They consider it irrelevant. The orientation programme is very much expedient in the process of your university preparation. In fact, it's the introductory stage. The orientation unfolds the university curriculum, and helps you to be familiar with campus and campus authorities. A prospectus might be available, but the prospectus does not, sometimes, give detailed explanation, and is not open to questions. During the orientation, you learn more about the different faculties, departments and fields of study, which helps you truly understand the various courses. That aids you to make proper decisions relating to speciality. All students register for their various courses at the start of every academic year. So, as a freshman, you need to know your campus before commencing that process. The orientation also helps in that regard. No matter your background, please try to reside on campus, if it applies to your University; this activity helps you become a family. On completion of my orientation, I was already familiar with campus, especially the administrative buildings, which made my initial registration process faster and movement around campus easier.

Social Activities

During academic pursuit, student interaction and recreation are essential to evade mental stress, but that should be mitigated and not in the negative. In my day, social distraction started, most times, during the orientation period. Heads, and other executive members, of social clubs on campus approached, invaded and cajoled freshmen into their membership procedures. Social clubs were officially registered on campus and their events recognized by University Authorities. But, in spite of the legality, authorities closely monitored their activities both in and out of campus. The problem with social clubs is not just about being a member, but with the activities of the membership. As students, you must interact at a cordial and permissible level to humanity. Violent and other inhuman practices must be eliminated. 'Sexual promiscuity' is the hidden aim of many social clubs on campus, but this is cunningly presented to intellectually-focused students, especially freshmen, so they do not see their tutelage being negatively affected. Most of the social clubs wheedle students into an extravagant release of funds, like paying enormous annual dues and contributing to hosting parties. Students must refrain from vices like alcoholism, sexual immorality and immoral songs.

The amount of time spent on Social Media Platforms is conspicuously alarming.

Students engage themselves on WhatsApp, Facebook, Twitter, Instagram and other social media. Some make beneficial use of it, like posting brain-teasing questions that improve their academic strengths. Others post educationally-profiting articles and carry out other forms of healthy communication. But some students engage in pornographic interactions that help distort their educational path. You can use the Internet to download video and audio recordings on academic tutorials. This would help you master courses. As a student, please allow your social media participation to remain a value-added activity to your educational pursuit.

Refuse to be distracted! Remain focused! Remain determined!

Medical Examination

Your mental strength is greatly influenced by your medical capacity. Many universities, if not all, conduct medical examinations as part of their admissions procedures. That prepares students for hard work. You need to be in good shape to begin university work. If your institution doesn't provide one, personally seek a private doctor to perform your medical tests, and hence diagnoses. This must be a continual practice. I recommend monthly or tri-monthly medical checks. You might consider this expensive, but one encounter with a lethal disease is enough to help you understand that the perceived financial gain is truly a financial loss. A medical doctor or any related practitioner, or dietician, must be sought for advice on diet - not all diets are ideal for all situations. That is to say, during study period, you should know the type of food to feed on; including drinks and solid victuals. You must know the types and time of diets. Do not drug or intoxicate yourself. Good and constant exercises, alongside medication, must be part of your doctor's recommendation. Remember, your physical strength largely depends on the state of your immune system. Bad health reduces your working ability and sometimes makes it non-effective. University authorities should begin to enforce medical examinations as part of university admissions procedures. It's better to gain knowledge of the medical status of prospective students, which would help you properly manage them. Even after admissions, I advise you do it annually - at the start of every academic year.

Relationship with Colleagues

Interaction with fellow freshmen and continuing students should generally begin during the orientation period, but must not terminate at that level. Your fellow students should be viewed, not just as mates, but as true biological relations. This enhances your familiarity and efficiency on campus. At the university, especially Fourah Bay College, notices are sometimes posted on boards and walls in concealed locations, and sometimes you are unaware. But with good relationships, you would be intimated. Yes, I had a tight class mate, Dominic During, in third year, but probably I couldn't have missed that 'Communications I' examination if I had a healthy tie with other colleagues in class. Many accused me of pride, but I was just an introverted type and very selective in friendship. Sharing stuff, like educational materials, is also essential. In Africa, especially Sierra Leone, it's hard to see students who are totally complete, lacking nothing, no matter how wealthy. Having the required finance is good, but availability is another hurdle. So sharing helps you forge ahead and save time. Some students are introverts, but employ your introversion prudently. Don't remain isolated!

Relationship with Lecturers and Other University Authorities

Student-Lecturer relationship is a prime-mover in the field of academia. There should be that Mentor-Mentee relationship. Lecturers must be respected! You don't need to lobby. Depend on your brain, but respect plays a great role. When you need legal academic assistance from him or clarity on specific tuition, don't hesitate to meet him. Remain humble and accept your lecturer as the boss, as far as the classroom is concerned. If you think you hurt a lecturer, apologize in person before it gets worse. In situations where he cannot grant you audience, talk to colleagues of his; preferably close friends or other lecturers of the same faculty or department. Not in the form of complaint, as they all are compatriots, but in humility. Lecturers should not see their students as enemies, but as true biological relations. It's normal for lecturers to like brilliant or hardworking students, but must remain impartial in the discharge of their duties. Favouritism and malice must not be a practice in academic institutions. Some lecturers see brilliant students as threats, victimizing them and all sorts. This practice must be terminated at Universities. On the other hand, if a student is engaged in activities detesting to a lecturer, he must face the student, advising him. To the student, no matter how brilliant you think you are, desist from challenging a lecturer, except on academic principles, but that should be done with respect and acknowledge him as a mentor, even if he doesn't teach you directly. However, as a student, you have the right to make official complaint if you think you're unfairly treated. Lecturers must cease from dating students, to maintain their respect. Like lecturers, other University Authorities must also be highly respected as they also can influence your academic achievement. Remember, getting through a University is not just about making A s, but your behaviour counts as well – you can be expelled for reckless attitude.

We had experienced lecturers, but among them was a newly-graduated tutor who lectured us on Applied Mechanics in second-year. I believe that guy was brilliant, but his first appearing period in the lecture room was insufficient to get him a protected confidence. He was somehow jittery in class, and hence couldn't deliver well, which earned him continual disrespect among mentees. Sometimes students would engage in giggling practices, as he unfolded his mechanical analyses - that got him agitated. That act continued and when we walked into his examination hall, the questions set by that tutor, appeared to be beyond our ken. Some students bowed their heads and others were swapping answer-scripts containing solutions they couldn't buy. The Lecturer marked, submitted the grades and travelled overseas. Our grades were revealed and I could remember two students who got 'C' and 'C-'. I got a 'D' and the bulk emerged with 'E s' and 'F s'. When the results were posted, the 'E s' and 'F s' translated into 'A s' and 'B s'. My 'D' remained 'D' and the other passes as well. So when others looked at those results, they would say the students with the A s and B s are the better. The lecturer who initially taught and examined us travelled abroad either on further studies or otherwise – but he ceded his appointment. He was then replaced by another lecturer who demanded money from students who wanted to improve on their grades, especially those who failed. Students always desire to make better grades. So whenever some see opportunities, they go for it. But if you're a student, desist from such practices, as it would destroy your academic foundation and show-up during practice. I want to believe it happens in other parts of Africa and even in other continents. Remember, the field of academia or the lecture room must not be viewed as a platform where money or sleeping with a Lecturer becomes a criterion to make good grades.

Get Ready For Examinations

The goal of fulfilling all other conditions at the university is to enable you go through your examinations successfully. Examinations are inevitable in academic chase. You need to execute proper planning procedures to achieve maximum results. With hard work from the initial stage, you become familiar with your course, but special arrangements have to be made as examinations approach, especially when the timetable is posted. You need to translate your normal study timetable in accordance with the posted examinations timetable. Not, essentially, in order of occurrence, but how you can handle them in terms of performance. Sometimes, you work very hard during lecture periods, but with bad revision procedures, you achieve reduced grades. You need to revise well. Teamwork is very essential. With teamwork, you exchange ideas and save time. At the end of every topic, solve related problems, especially from past papers and textbooks. That exposes you to the format of questions and prepares you for examinations, though you need to apply your Intelligence Quotient. Hang around the examinations hall about thirty minutes ahead, as permitted by your university regulations. Face the examinations with confidence, believe you would make it and attain a height of excellence.

Unwitting Personal Initiation

Isaiah 47:13-14 says, 'Thou art wearied in the multitude of thy counsels. Let now the astrologers, the stargazers, the monthly prognosticators, stand up, and save thee from these things that shall come upon thee. Behold, they shall be as stubble; the fire shall burn them; they shall not deliver themselves from the power of the flame: there shall not be a coal to warm at, nor fire to sit before it.' - KJV.

The Almighty God opposes Astrology. Sometimes, students continually wallow in ignorance as they trade their academic destinies. Unknowingly, they entangle themselves, destroying their psychological foundation. When I was a student, we used to read newspaper articles, magazines, and even the Internet, investigating future happenings, especially in relationships. These normally appeared in the form of Zodiac interpretations. Horoscope predictions are presented in an intellectual fashion, but have occult attachments. They're truly related to hidden Satanic divinity. I am not fighting with the truth or falsity of Astrology because demons always present duplications of Godly elements. In this sense, I am talking about the effects of horoscopes on students. Students get so glued to these astrological revelations, and unintentionally initiate themselves in two forms:

(i) Physical Personal Initiation

When you begin reading through zodiac interpretations, you are influenced to depend on them, and at some point, living without them becomes hard. This is identical to sorcery, but appears in an academic form, so the negative side becomes hidden. When you read through a zodiac publication which tells you that you'll quarrel with your fiancée on a particular date, you prepare to meet her in counteraction - you find ways to bring it to pass. Even if your partner does something that was not supposed to lead to a fight, you try to fulfil the zodiac prediction. This serves as a distraction, because when your human foundation is distorted, you could hardly execute your coursework successfully. When I was engaged in zodiac readings, I was a Scorpio. I became so addicted to it that my youthful social life was largely influenced by it. So stay away from zodiac interpretations.

(ii) Spiritual Personal Initiation

Continual involvement in zodiac practices leads to demonic initiation without your knowing. You establish a soul tie with powers of darkness, which develops into a normal occurrence. Demons begin to control your emotions. You get attached to reading the zodiac. When you read their explanations, they remotely control you until you make it happen. They cause you to become bitter against people. Whenever you see people related to horoscope interpretations, you develop hate. Sometimes they manipulate you to misconstrue the zodiac message, all to make your relationship with people deformed. This negatively influences your study life and could lead to delay or failure. So desist from reading information related to zodiac charts or any foretelling event.

Remain Prayerful

Many problems encountered in life are spiritual. Working in keeping with the outlined admonitions would remain nullified with the operation of opposing forces.

In Genesis 2:7, Scripture says, 'And the Lord God formed man of the dust of the ground, and breathed into his nostrils the breath of life; and man became a living soul'. In 1 Thessalonians 5:23, Paul says, '...and I pray God your whole spirit and soul and body be preserved...". Humans are spiritual beings, with souls living in earthly vessels. A high percentage of students, especially unbelievers, attend to the corporeal needs, neglecting the spiritual. The veiled man, which comprises the Spirit and Soul, controls the unveiled man, which is the Body. The veiled man survives without the unveiled man, but the unveiled man cannot exist without the veiled man. So if you ignore the veiled man, slowly every area of you begins to die, including your education.

Prayer is communicating with the Creator of the Universe, executed by the Spirit. Prayer is a command! In Jeremiah 33:3, The LORD says, 'Call unto me and I will answer thee...'. The essence of fulfilling all commandments, in Scriptures, is to establish a healthy communication with our Heavenly Father. Students need to pray before applying to the university, for God to reveal their assignment. As I discussed earlier, your field of study is a function of your talent and assignment. Friends can help you uncover your talent, but your assignment can only be revealed by The Almighty God. In Secondary School, you can be good in sciences and emerge with all As, which qualifies for any scientific path of your choice. You might have a passion for Engineering, but probably God wants you to become a medical doctor – that's why you need to pray for divine revelation of your career path. In Matthew 21:22, Jesus says 'And all things, whatsoever ye shall ask in prayer, believing, ye shall receive.' When you pray, you should believe that The Almighty God would answer. But you have to be sensitive to discern that. And that would only happen when you have a healthy relationship with The Almighty God or else you get deceived by the Devil. God talks to man through visions, dreams, man, silently, or can even guide you into making the right decision. One of the major ways God talks to me is through dreams. Humanly, I was able to identify my talents, with the aid of friends and tutors, but my Writing Assignment was revealed to me in a dream. In the dream, during a personal thirty-day prayer-and-fasting act, I saw a very big pen, and instantly the Writing Assignment occurred to me. We need to be constantly talking with our Maker, for protection and other relevant issues, to enable us transform our preordained dreams into reality. Communications is a two-way process. In simple terms, it's the transmission and reception of information, through a channel, governed by a protocol. The spirit realm is the channel, whilst the protocol refers to Christian Principles. It means communicating with God depends on your relationship with Him, which is guarded by the spiritual protocol. When you violate Christian principles, communications between you and God become distorted. The spirit realm can be obstructed by demons, but as long as you do not violate the protocol, you would remove any Satanic interruption. The Almighty God says, 'Call unto Me and I will answer...' So if you call upon Him and he doesn't answer, then something is wrong. Demonic operations are invisible. When demonic forces operate, it doesn't just happen. They create ways to relate your problem to the physical world. They would cause you to violate at least one of the related principles outlined, and make you and other students believe the problem is related to the natural. In my case, I was distracted from my coursework, and it made me sometimes forget I was a student. When it was revealed and I kept praying, I started working hard. When the Devil realized that, he established a bitter relationship between me and my lecturer. Mr.

Thorlu Bangura liked me so much. In third year, he offered us tuition on Electronics, Microcomputer Engineering and Digital Systems. And I was doing very well in his modules, especially Digital Systems and Microcomputer Engineering. In fact, I got an 'A' in Digital Electronics, referred to as Electronics Engineering II, taught by Dr. Bah, to promote me to third year. So my digital foundation was very strong. Mr. Bangura was very fond of me, pulling my leg whenever we met. But he was demonically transformed, and hated me as a real enemy. He never made up with me until after my graduation. But remember, there's nothing prayer cannot change. I prayed with dedication and my steps were guided by The Holy Ghost.

When I travelled to Ghana for the second time, I stayed with Moinya. Clarissa later left the hostel and relocated to Tesanon. And so we had less time together than when we were in the same area. At some point, I started feeling distant from her. When I was growing up, I liked dating a girl in my neighbourhood, even if it wasn't for a serious relationship. So when Clarissa relocated, I felt lonely sometimes and that inspired me to establish a casual relationship. I started cheating on Clarissa. The new girl was in my neighbourhood, and used to pay me visits in Clarissa's absence. One afternoon, she entered my bedroom and made herself convenient on the bedside cupboard, which was her normal sitting position. Suddenly, I heard something drop on the floor with a very high force. I turned and realized it was my casual girlfriend. Initially, I thought she was epileptic, but when she started fighting in the air, pulling and throwing items, causing disorder in the entire room, I realized it was something more than epilepsy. I tried stopping her, but the more I tried, the more she increased in physical strength. I couldn't control her. I used to attend Church services, but my Christian life was lukewarm. At some point, she was off the floor and rushed towards the exit door, but I managed to lock it. Spiritually, I was premature and didn't know what to do, so I shouted 'Moinya', as the fight continued. Moinya rushed into the room. As she arrived in, she knew it was a demonic operation. The girl was on the floor, physically fighting with the air and instantly, Moinya started pleading the Blood of Jesus. She didn't touch her. In a moment, the whole atmosphere returned pacific.

When she totally came round, I said to her, 'Darling, you know I love you, right? I know it wasn't your fault, but please tell me what happened, okay?' For a start, she was shy. But I pampered her and she smiled. 'Samou', she started, 'I picked-up a ring sometime ago while walking along the beach. When I went to bed, at night, I had a dream of a white man claiming to be my husband. I replied, "but I don't even know you", and he continued, "but you have my ring already, we're married". Suddenly, I woke up in daze. I ran straight to the beach, dropped the ring and safely walked back home. The following night, he re-appeared in my dream. I informed him about the return of his ring, but he declined accepting it, emphasizing I must place it at the exact location I picked it from. How could that be possible? He underscored that we're married and would not let me go. Since that night, he'd been appearing in my dreams, sometimes sleeping with me. That practice separated me and my then-boyfriend because he threatened me not to have any earthly relationship. For a long time, I had no time for an intimate love affair with any physical man. Later, I started praying and attended Church meetings because I realized it was evil and not in my interest. And in those periods, I had no time for a relationship related to romance. I was truly focused on God. The dream ceased, but whenever I got into any earthly romantic relationship, it resumed. I then made a resolution to totally focus on God and not to have an affair anymore with any man. This had been my position for the past few years and I was fine. But when I saw you for the first time, I was strongly attracted to you. I couldn't understand. I couldn't control myself, but fell in love with you. I recalled the consequences, but took the risk because I didn't want to let go of you. And when we made love for the first three times, he warned me, but I didn't listen. Even though I continued praying, look at what happened? And today, he vowed that if you don't stay away from me, he would make you impotent'.

I stood up in great fear, with goose flesh all over me, and sweating; my heartbeat increased in rate. Sometimes, we treat occurrences trivially until we face them in the real world. That was someone I had an affair with. I had started falling in love with her, but needed nobody to advise me after that devilish demonstration. I retired from her, but she continued her visits. Whenever I saw her coming home, I got dressed up and went out, even if it wasn't premeditated. Whenever I met her on the way, I ignored her and took a different path. When we met by chance, I just said 'hi' and duplicated an action of urgency to put her advances on hold. That was real pain, even to me! I didn't know how to deal with demons. And, in fact, I wasn't ready to become a committed Christian. I was intimidated by the reality of her utterance and decided to terminate that Satanic relationship. She kept complaining to my sister, but I made her comprehend it was in the interest of the both of us and we got truly separated. Demonic operations are real! Demons do exist! We tend to be stubborn until we face it. In many cases, people only consider relationship gains, ignoring the losses. But don't permit your being to swim in a dark pool.

In another situation, during my days at Fourah Bay College, I met with another girl who was not a student of my institution. We had a chat and, in principle, she became my girlfriend. We made an agreement for me to pick her up and pay me a visit. But as the time approached, I got truly tired and didn't go. Afterwards, we met on the street and I apologized for not picking her up. We made another appointment and again I didn't show up. As soon as the time approached, I felt weakened again. Again, I apologized, but that time it was on the phone. And we made a third appointment. That was to pick her up late in the evening to come home. And for the third time, I failed. First thing the next morning, I gave her a call for another apology. Her ringing tone sounded for some time, but she didn't pick up. Suddenly, I heard a masculine voice talking to me through her phone. Guess what? It was her father, intimating to me she passed away at home that night. I was shocked and for a while couldn't say a word, as my tummy intermittently wobbled. In a jittery mood, the handset almost fell off my hand, and I could sense great disappointment from her father's voice. Based on our appointment, she was supposed to spend that night at my residence. Imagine what could have happened? Her father said she died of tummy pains. The same morning, I left home to see her family. I had never been there, but her father gave me the description. On the way, I passed by a friend's house, Anthony Sinnah, who resided in her neighbourhood, but wasn't sure if he knew her. I informed him about the incident and that I was going to see her family. But Anthony strongly advised me not to go there, even though I wanted to. Later, I heeded to his advice and went back home.

The Almighty God loves us so much and always tries to protect us. But sometimes our stubbornness gets us into trouble.

In those two incidents, my academic destiny could have been destroyed, or deformed, because if that girl had died in my bedroom, I might have been locked up - probably for life - or even face a death penalty. If I had been impotent, my academic journey could have been immensely obstructed, as my mind would have been in turmoil. Yes, I could have been delivered by our Lord Jesus, but how long it would have taken, I can't say, because sometimes God can allow you to go through situations to get you in good shape. That witchcraft ritual was even succeeding against me because I was into fornication. I prayed fervently, but the fornication kept me in an undulating motion. When I abstained and prayed, I saw progress. But whenever I got into fornication, I noticed the trouble. Your body is the Temple of The Holy Ghost. So when you defile the Temple, you aggrieve The Holy Spirit and you establish a barrier between you and The Almighty God. So when you pray, your prayer becomes nullified by your fornication. Always remember, fornication can destroy your academic destiny. It can destroy your destiny.

■■■

CHAPTER X

The True Success Equation

Many around the globe misconstrue the concept of success. They believe success is all about pecuniary achievement. They believe success is all about money. Success, in simple terms, is achieving a set goal, or just an achievement. Because sometimes you don't set yourself a goal, but it happens. If I wish to have a car and I obtain it, I am successful. If I desire to be a Pastor and I become, I am successful. If I dream to be an Electrical Engineer and I achieve it, I am successful. If I desire to prophesy and I prophesy, I am successful. Now, let's look at success from four different perspectives.

1. Success in a goal - Irrespective of path

This is an achievement in a specific case. It refers to success through whatever means. Whether you steal, or achieve it through hard work, it doesn't matter. You don't care about the route, as long as you made it. For example, if I need a pair of shoes, no matter how I get it, all I care about is to get it. If I want to travel to the United States, whether I go through Brussels or London, it doesn't matter. All I care about is to get there. This is success in specific cases, irrespective of route.

2. Success on a general scale - Irrespective of path

This refers to achievement in goals generally, irrespective of the route taken. Again, this doesn't care about how you get to the point. Whether through dishonest means, it doesn't matter. It talks about success in your lifetime. Your career or whatever you end up as in life. For instance, if you end up as a renowned businessman – whether you get involved in fraud or not – you are successful. This refers to lifetime achievement or success, irrespective of the path taken.

3. Success in a goal - According to God's Will

This refers to success in a specific goal, according to God's purpose. It is an achievement by man in specific cases as inspired by God. It's not achieved or obtained through fraud or malpractice. It is genuine, and it's the real will of God. For instance, if you were designed for a particular career and during the course, you studied hard, prayed and went through an examination, without any form of malpractice, you're successful. This refers to success in a specific case according to God's will.

4. Success on a general scale - According to God's Will

You can succeed in whatever form, whether according to the will of The Heavenly Father or not. But this form of success refers to achieving your ultimate goal according to God's will. This refers to veritable prosperity - driven by God. You can succeed by merit, but not according to the will of God. Achievement by merit according to the will of God is your assignment on this planet. This is the success we will be discussing: God's earthly plan for Man - True Success.

True Success is discussed in relation to Man. As we discussed earlier, Man is a spirit, with a soul, living in a physical vessel – the body. The soul is the interface between the body and spirit. The soul relays information from the Spirit to the body and vice-versa. When you want to think, you use your soul. When you want to physically walk, you use your body. When you want to talk with God, you use your spirit. But they all work in unison. So, in spite of his mortality, man exhibits immortal characteristics, as well. Based on these facts, and principles, I derived an equation, referred to as 'The True Success Equation'. This equation was designed for students, but applies to all sectors of life. Stated below is the **True Success Equation** - the apparatus to get you to your maximum preordained height. Study it well, comprehend it and apply. The equation is given as follows:

$$S_T = T + E + P \quad \text{--------1}$$

Where S_T = True Success
           T = Talent
           E = Effort
           P = Prayer

The above equation can be restated as

True Success = Talent + Effort + Prayer ------2

Let me help you define the parameters of the equation.

Talent (T)

Talent is an inbuilt potential. It is the natural ability inherited from birth. I did not say inherited from parents, I said inherited from birth; you were born with it. It can be inherited from parents, but the origin is God. An offspring can have a talent both parents do not possess. For instance, if you add equal portions of black and white oil paints, you end up with grey. It can be derived from them, but their amalgam can produce a unique output. You do not earn talent, you do not work for it - it's just there. It's a gift from God. When you fully utilize your talent, 'True Success' belongs to you. But you can be full of talent and depart this planet without fulfilling your assignment. So talent all by itself doesn't help, which leads to the concept of 'Effort'.

Effort (E)

This is the physical strength you impart into an activity, event or project. Talent is a gift. But when you identify your talent, you have to trigger it, you have to nurture it. You need to develop it to the maximum point. This is only achieved by applying 'Effort' to specific situations. You have to constantly practise and dedicate yourself to it. This talks about hard work. You can be in possession of all the talents in the world, but if you don't develop them, they end up being wasted. So at the point you recognize your talent, work must be done. You must apply 'Effort'. Activate your talent, incubate it, nurture it and rise to your maximum height.

Talent and Effort might sometimes not work, but there's a third parameter which would enable them work at all times. That parameter is Prayer.

Prayer (P)

Prayer is the tool to erasing demonic tags. Satan applies camouflaged techniques to keep you away from, or walk you out of, your assignment. He would always attach natural occurrences to situations, to help divert your attention and let your trouble appear physical. Sometimes, you can perfectly identify your talent and fully apply effort, but without prayer, you would just be flogging a dead horse. Well, talent and effort can work very well, but because this world is wicked, humans can be demonically possessed, and because of that, Man becomes unpredictable. Demonic agents have no respect for biological relationships, let alone ordinary friendships. Even loved individuals like friends, brothers, sisters, parents and guardians can hunt you, when they carry demonic spirits. But with continual prayer, demonic obstruction would be countered. Remember, prayer is the spiritual strength you add to your talent. It is the 'spiritual effort'.

Recall -----1, 'The True Success Equation'

$S_T = T + E + P$

This can be restated as

$S_T - T = E + P$ ----1A

This implies trying to truly succeed without talent, just by applying effort and prayer. Things don't just happen by chance. God deposited gifts into every man because He knew the needs of the world, and designed different men to attend to different needs. With just prayer, your efforts might be wasted. Pray for God to reveal your talent if you can't identify it, before applying effort. True success would not be achieved just by praying and applying effort, talent must be involved.

Again, ----1 can be restated as

$S_T - E = T + P$ ----1B

This depicts trying to succeed truly just by prayer and talent. No matter how you pray; if you do not activate your talent, if you do not apply that physical strength, you would not get to your maximum height. For instance, you can have a talent in mathematics, but if you do not get the right tuition, how could you benefit from it? If you do not interact with your notes or do research, how would you make it? If you do not practise by solving problems, how would you master it? You can't just lie in bed praying. You must get up and apply effort.

----1 can also be re-written as:

$S_T - P = T + E$ ----1C

This means pursuing 'True Success' without prayer.

Sometimes, trying to truly succeed without prayer might seem to work, but you must pray for three major reasons. Firstly, you pray for The Almighty God to reveal your assignment. Secondly, you pray to preclude demonic limitations. Satanic obstructions may come, but with prayer you would overcome. And thirdly, you pray to maximize your potential. The Almighty God called Bezaleel, of the tribe of Judah, and filled him with His Spirit which imparted wisdom, Understanding and Knowledge into him to do all manner of Workmanship – see Exodus 31:1-5. Wisdom comes from The Almighty God. So if you desire to do extraordinary events, you need the Spirit of God. Even when you know your assignment, even when there's no demonic interruption, you pray for God to increase you in fixing complicated issues. The Talent you have was giving to you by The Almighty God. So if you want to make the best use of it, make God your Chief Consultant.

----------------1 can be re-arranged as

$S_T - P - T = E$ ----1D

This implies pursuing True Success just by applying Effort, ignoring Talent and Prayer. Coincidentally, this might seem to work sometimes. But working outside your Talent and Assignment can be frustrating.

-------------1 can further be re-stated as

$S_T - P - E = T$ ----1E

This represents pursuing True Success, neglecting Prayer and Effort. Sometimes, students lazily pursue their academic dream. Some recognize their Talent, but do not work hard to make it happen or excel. Others do not pray. So spiritually and physically, they apply no Effort. This is eternally destructive, if not corrected.

------------1 can be further re-stated as

$S_T - E - T = P$ ----1F

This explains pursuing True Success just by praying, ignoring Talent and Effort. I believe in divine interventions. Prayer reveals your Assignment. It helps preclude satanic obstructions, and maximizes your potential. But you must activate and develop your Talent. You must employ your Talent and apply Effort.

At the University, I had the Talent. I applied Effort, but only succeeded when I prayed effectively. Prayer is powerful, but 1 John 5:14 says, 'And this is the confidence that we have in Him, that, if we ask anything according to His Will, He heareth us' (KJV). So if you don't pray according to The Will of The Almighty God, your prayer would remain questionable.

From this discourse, you can see that talent, effort and prayer are the factors on which true success depends. Talent is directly related to the Soul. Effort is directly related to the body. And Prayer is directly related to the spirit. So for man to truly succeed, the body, soul and spirit must involve.

So, identify your 'Talent', apply 'Effort', 'Pray', and be at your best.

■■■

CHAPTER XI

Chase It!

Some students are intimidated to challenge certain courses, or projects, even when they meet all criteria, due to incertitude or mediocrity. We're living in an age of excellence, a time to be at your best, a period not to settle for the minute. Man was designed, specifically, to dominate. He was created to rule the Earth, and so there's no need to be in a relegating position. When God made man, He deposited, into him, everything he needed to exist on Earth. Those deposits were hidden in the form of talents, but one of the greatest troubles is for man to identify those talents. Let us now discuss some ways to help humanly recognize your talent.

Talent Identification

Your Hobby

A hobby is an activity you engage in, especially during your leisure or recreational period. It is what you like doing. Your hobby can be, or be related to, your talent. Sometimes, you just find yourself doing something, in many cases during your 'free' time. Soccer was a hobby, and every time I played people would applaud my doing it. But I didn't pursue it.

I liked helping people with mathematical problems. When I saw someone struggle with mathematics, I would step in and help. Sometimes at home, I would just pick-up A4-sized sheets of paper and start working on some mathematics – doing equations and more. Even when I discussed general issues, I liked using mathematical analogies.

When I was at the university, I liked sending people text messages, especially my girlfriends, and some colleagues started referring to me as a poet, which helped me uncover my writing talent. Remember, a hobby can also become an addiction. You can have multiple events you like engaging in. So think about your hobbies and investigate those recreational activities.

What Do People Admire You Doing?

You don't only rely on personal judgement to help identify your talent. Everybody has a potential which is, most times, revealed to other people. People who observe you, or people you work with. Critics are sometimes malicious, but when it becomes universal, take it into consideration and act on it. It is unlikely that people would criticize you generally for what you are good at. I had a girlfriend during my university days who was a student of the Milton Margai College of Education and Technology. She was Alice. One of the ways I used to entice girls was through text messaging. I used to send that girl romantic messages on a daily basis, most times in the morning, and sometimes at night. During a particular period, I stopped sending messages because I got distracted by something else. So one day she gave me a call and said 'Samou, my brother would kill me.' I asked 'why?' and she revealed that her brother was using the texts I sent her, to send his girlfriend loving info every day. So when I ceased, he was deprived, and his girlfriend kept bothering him about messages and he didn't let her know it was someone else's messages he was using. I laughed out loud and continued messaging to save her brother from embarrassment, but that didn't last, as I broke up with the girl later. As an Electrical Engineering student, friends always admired my writings to an extent that one off-campus friend asked whether I was a Law student at Fourah Bay College. All that helped unveil my writing talent.

What Do You Enjoy Doing?

Sometimes, you don't always do it, but every time you do it, you enjoy it. What you enjoy doing can also help you identify your talent. I was glued to my mobile phone, but I enjoyed text messaging more than oral conversation. Many times when I talk with people on a cell phone, I find ways to initiate texts, just to get myself writing. During my initial days at the University, I met an African-American girl, called Iman. She was born in the United States of America, but her father was born in Sierra Leone. In America, her father met her mother, who was also an African-American. I believe the girl's Mum was also born in America because she had a very negative perception about Africa. According to Iman, her Mum thought Africa was full of beasts, and didn't want her daughter to even step on the soils of Africa. But her father was determined to let his daughter know her paternal origin and they travelled to Sierra Leone. That was the first time she stepped out of America. When I met that girl in Freetown, we liked each other and exchanged cell phone numbers. We started talking on the phone, and in few days she travelled to an Eastern Sierra Leonean town called Kenema, together with her father. Her father's ancestors originated from Giema, a village close to Kenema. Then I fought to keep our conversation via text messaging, except for a few occasions. As we continued, she recognized my writing skill, and from her responses, I could sense she was really moved, especially with my thought pattern. She would send me messages and I replied with instantaneous romanticism. From her words, I began to feel the ambience of a distant dating. At some point, she couldn't hold it back, and without remorse, she tendered a request, demanding my travel to meet her in Kenema. University had just re-opened and that was a week of registration. But many times, we used the first week to register and sometimes, for two weeks, we had no lectures. So I informed her I was registering, and when I realized there were no tuition going on, I quickly travelled to Kenema. My late father had a house in Kenema, so it was easy for me. I spent a few days with Iman, and went back to the university. I was using my writing skill for fun, but it was during those processes I recognized my writing talent.

I am an Electrical Engineer, but every time I write, I enjoy doing it. I never get bored with writing. I always enjoy writing about anything. But now, I don't use my writing skill on activities that glorify the Devil.

What Do You Excel In?

Whenever you do some things, you excel. Other times, you don't even want to do something, but every time you do it, you get positive results. When I was writing my private Ordinary Level exams, I was outstanding in Mathematics. Whenever we were taught on a specific topic, I mastered it the next day. It got to a point that our teacher started sending me to the blackboard to help my mates. Every pupil in the class respected me for excellence in Mathematics. In another instance, a boy in my neighbourhood struggled on a problem in Mathematics. Someone advised him to meet me, but he was reluctant because, to him, I wasn't studious, and always attended parties and night clubs. Many times, he saw me moving around with girls, so he thought I couldn't be good, as I appeared not to be serious in his eyes. At that time, I was doing my A-Level course at the Sierra Leone Grammar School, and on

Monday morning, after struggling with his homework right through the weekend, he finally met me. He was supposed to submit his work that morning. It was a problem on construction and I was dressing up for school. I looked through the problem while putting on my shirt and requested his compass, pencil, ruler and set squares. To his surprise, I spent less than a minute to solve it. He used his protractor and ruler to verify the angles and dimensions - they were accurate. The boy was just staring at me, without saying a word as he retreated home. So you excel based on external judgement, driven by proofs. That can be your talent.

What Do You Have Passion For?

There are certain things you're enthusiastic about, but you don't do them, probably due to lack of opportunities. This is an enormous problem, especially in Africa, specifically Sierra Leone, where people are restricted to certain courses or careers. In other cases, you actually do them. This is not talking about instantaneous zest, but an activity you have a burning desire to always do. You always get urge to involve in it. Even if you are engaged in something else, you create ways to walk into such activities. I have a passion for writing. Even when I stayed on site in the provinces, with huge electrical responsibilities, I always find time to do articles, most times on Facebook. I always get that burning desire to write.

Identifying talent is a combination of factors, and it's a process. You don't just consider a factor and say, 'this is my talent.' And it's determined over a period – not just in a single activity. From personal observation, talent starts showing up between the ages of 0-5 years, and fully manifest within the period of 5-18 years, generally.

So I believe the above mentioned points would help you, to a large extent, humanly identify that in-built ability – that deposit from The Almighty God.

Many cannot make a distinction between talent and skill. We will now see the difference.

Talent vs Skill

Many times, it becomes difficult to distinguish between talent and skill. But we must fight not to replace talent with skill. They are closely related, but not identical. Talent is a hidden skill. When talent is developed, it becomes a skill. But, even though you have the talent, if you do not develop it, you would not have the skill. Skill is a cultivated technique - knowing how to do something. But you can be skilled in something that is not your talent. This is achieved as a result of practice. It comes with experience. When you constantly do something, you become skilled in it with time. But you struggle to master it, because you are not naturally cut out for that. When you work in your talent, you don't struggle to comprehend. You don't struggle to excel. Yes, you need to work hard, you need to apply effort. But you don't struggle to understand the principles. In the Engineering Faculty, at Fourah Bay College, students used to do General Engineering for the first two years, and then separate into their different disciplines which included Civil, Electrical and Electronics, and Mechanical/Maintenance. So Lecturers must focus more on class participation than written examinations, to see how students respond to tuition, especially when new concepts are taught. And try to see how students apply principles taught to solve problems in class. At the Sierra Leone Grammar School, when I just got promoted to the Upper Sixth form before the political upheaval, our Pure and Applied Mathematics tutors Mr. George Kobba and the late Mr. Bull would post problems on the Blackboard, and we would compete as to who would first come up with a correct solution. That helped us remain in readiness, and improved our mathematical skills. And talents showed up because the problems, I believe, were new to us. Homework was good, but that would only help if students could defend their work in class, as some students duplicated solutions of others. And you would use that, coupled with their examination grades, to determine which discipline they could get into. A student can have a strong desire for Civil Engineering, but if he finds himself excelling in Electricals, then that's his discipline. High School Tutors should apply the same principles before pupils get into university. Talent only benefits society when it becomes a skill. Some also confuse talent and Intelligence Quotient. We shall now examine them.

Talent vs IQ

Talent is not the same as Intelligence Quotient – IQ. IQ defines your general reasoning strength relative to others of your age, whilst Talent refers to your reasoning capacity in a specific field. Researcher Alfred Binet, who lived in France around 1904, defined Intelligence Quotient as a ratio of your Mental Age to your Chronological Age, multiplied by 100. He multiplied by 100 to get a round figure. According to him, your Chronological Age is your Biological Age – your Age from birth. And your Mental Age is your thinking capacity, relative to other ages. For instance, if all five-year-olds are only supposed to be able to read and sing, and you're five years and can only sing but can't read, then your Mental Age is less than your Chronological Age. Further, if all four-year-olds are only expected to sing, then your Mental Age is four.

Mathematically, Intelligence Quotient can be expressed as:

IQ = (Mental Age/Chronological Age) X 100

If we make Mental Age = MA and Chronological Age = CA, then

IQ = (MA/CA) X 100

Now, if we consider our Argument, Mental Age = 4 and Chronological Age = 5, which implies

MA = 4

CA = 5

So, substituting for MA and CA in the IQ Equation yields

IQ = (4/5) X 100

= 400/5

IQ = 80

Therefore, for our Argument, your IQ is 80. But your Mental Age is not supposed to be less than your Chronological Age. So for a normal average human, your Chronological Age should be equal to your Mental Age. So in our Argument, if the guy could only read and sing, then his Mental Age would be equal to 5. If we then substitute in our IQ Equation, we would get:

IQ = (5/5) X 100

= 1 X 100

IQ = 100

Hence, for a normal human, the IQ should be 100. That means your Chronological Age is equal to your Mental Age. However, if you are five, but do what six-year-olds are expected to do, then your Mental Age is 6, whilst your Chronological Age is 5. If we substitute in the IQ Equation, we get:

IQ = (6/5) X 100

   = 600/5

IQ = 120

In this case, your IQ is 120, which is above 100. Therefore, you are mentally advanced, because you do more than what is expected of your age. In our initial case, when the IQ was 80, you are considered mentally recessive, or mentally delayed, for you do less than what those of your age are expected to do. But IQ and Talent are interactive. IQ can be influenced by your state of mind, the environment and your type of diet. If you take an IQ test in a state of mental turmoil, you can perform poorer than you actually are. That's why, in determining IQ, you do it over a period of time and in many forms, including both Theory and Practice.

In Africa, especially Sierra Leone, many people do not gain access to food that helps develop the brain. Sometimes people eat the required food, but others say they live beyond their income. But the cost of eating the required diet is far less than the future gain. However, there are cheap foods rich in Nutrients. You just have to consult a Dietician. So, like Talent, IQ has to be developed. Two people can have the same Talent, but one performs better under identical conditions. Why? There is a difference in IQ. Some activities also help drop your IQ Level, hence reduced performance in Talent application, but you have to consult a specialist in that field – probably medical personnel. Some identify their talents, but do not accept them. Let's now discuss that.

Talent Acceptance

The problem in some parts of the world, especially in Africa, is not only to identify talent, but to accept it. When some discover their hidden potential, they don't honour it, because it doesn't match their dream. If everybody wants to wear a tie, if everybody wants to sit in an air-conditioned office, if nobody wants to be a subordinate – or if everybody wants to be a boss at once – who would lead? How could that be possible? We all want to reach our maximum heights, but there are processes, and my maximum height might not be your maximum.

Our God is a God of order and principles. Even in Heaven, there's hierarchy. People must realize talent is not only limited to the academic field. You can be an expert in cleaning floors. You can be a specialist in painting. In fact, in some countries, people pursue courses in those fields. If everybody accepts his talent, then the world would have a smooth sail. Accepting your talent would help you set up your own office, and you can become your own boss, if you so desire. Some accept their talents, but have problems developing them. We would now address that.

Talent Development

Another problem is with the development of talent. When you recognize and accept your talent, you don't just sit there, you activate it. You develop it to a visual level - a level seen and accepted by humanity. You must put it into practice. Talent must be applied. Development of talent is facilitated in application. Activate your hidden skills; put them into work. Utilize your potential in the interest of humanity. Some have talents, but the technological under-development, or the unavailability of facilities, is a huge hindrance, especially in Africa. Mediocrity is a universal epidemic, especially in Sierra Leone and other parts of Africa. Some do not go for excellence. They're only confined to a limited domain. Strive for excellence and stop being an 'ordinary man'.

Multi-Talents

Some are Multi-talented. Such people can do many things. They can excellently multi-task in different fields-of-study or profession. When you're Multi-talented, you have to be careful because sometimes you get confused as to what to do. In that regard, your assignment walks in, to help you make a decision. But many times, you get a major talent and a minor talent. And you always do better in your major than your minor. My family knew me for Mathematics, because I was a Science student in school. Actually, I didn't give much attention to English Language, as most Science pupils did. And they were truly surprised when they now know about the extent to which I write. I didn't study Arts at the university. I did not pursue a course in writing, but the talent was just there, and I personally developed it. So when you identify, accept and develop your talent, you're left with no other option but to chase your Assignment.

■■■

CHAPTER XII

Are You a Student?

Life as a student is very much unpredictable! Nobody soars to that level only to become a dropout. Nobody steps in to become a failure, nobody desires to delay. Every student who genuinely gains entrance into a university moves in with a passion to succeed within the required period – a passion to begin achieving his set dream.

I believe you've carefully read through my elucidation, identified the impeding factors, discovered ways to help you attain your pre-ordained heights and are now ready to 'chase it'. Probably, you've started chasing it already. The account you have just read is not just another story, but a true occurrence of me; a real testimony. It happened to me, and can happen to any student. That's what I am strongly fighting against. I humbly advise you to properly imbibe the contents of this book and truly emplace yourself at the university or any other Learning Institution. Your period of study could be your best, but it could also be your worst days, depending on your approach and other influencing circumstances. I spent three years in final year, the year that was supposed to be my last, something I was never prepared for. I don't want you to be another me! I don't want you to be another Samuel. I don't want you to be another victim.

You see, most of life's problems are spiritual, but many fail or delay to recognize that. Many students only depend on what they see - the physical. Some do not acquire that realization because they're ignorant of spiritual activities: they lack spiritual knowledge. Some are misled. As the first-born to succeed in Secondary School Sciences and enter University for a Bachelor's, I never thought of demonic metamorphosis, because I saw myself performing a family duty. From my account, there was an unsuccessful attempt to kidnap me in primary school, in which I could have been used for demonic rituals, mutilated or killed. In my secondary school days, my father lost his job abnormally, which seriously obstructed my Ordinary Level examinations preparation. At Advanced Level, there was political instability - an interregnum, which impeded my A-Level examinations plan to enter The College of

Medicine and Allied Health Sciences. At the university, there were attempts to exterminate me by road accidents. When I evaded all those tries, the Devil devised another strategy. I was distracted from my coursework. I was attacked in dreams. I was allocated a unique Design Project, which separated me and my supervisor. I only started realizing myself, and regained true focus on my academic work, after the revelation that I was demonically manipulated, and started praying fervently with the help of my pastor, Bishop Akintayo Sam-Jolly, General Overseer of the Living Word of Faith Outreach Ministries International, his wife Rev. Veralina Sam-Jolly and their assistant Pastor Rev. Joshua Alpha, who were used by God. The Devil recognized my focus and intensity of prayer, and didn't get tired, but made me have a bitter relationship with my lecturer who liked me so much. When my project design work was finally submitted, Satan did not relent, and he tried exterminating me before my graduation ceremony. I was struck with unprecedented illness. I used to get sick with malaria, but that attack was unique throughout my health status history. And about two days to our convocation ceremony, the Devil enacted his last attack – an SUV ran into a taxicab in which I was right at the back seat. The car creased right at the point I was seated. But I survived; untouched. I eluded all those attacks because of the Mercy and Grace of The Almighty God. By divine arrangement, The Almighty God used the late Dr. Joseph Kanu to work with me until all my graduation requirements were fulfilled. I graduated on 13th December, 2008, and unfortunately Dr. Joseph Kanu passed away on 10th February, 2009. I pray that The Almighty God helps him enjoy a peaceful eternity – in the Name of Jesus.

I know that at the university, especially at the average age, there're many excitements you wouldn't want to miss - the partying, clubbing, inter and intra-sex relationships, and more. But as you read from my account, I was a member of the most eminent social club, Quimanora, on campus: not only at Fourah Bay College, but country-wide as far as colleges and universities were concerned. I led all sorts of lives and dated so many girls, but never knew about that demonic manipulation, until its revelation. Humans can easily be manipulated by the Devil. You can be initiated into witchcraft with just a piece of cake or a bottle of drink. My former demon-possessed girlfriend just picked up a ring at the beach, and she got married to a demon – a white man. Be spiritually-minded! No matter how smart or hard-working you might be, demonic manipulation can cause you to do anything out of your control. It can get you into smoking ten packets of cigarettes, a day, when you never knew the smell of a stick. It can cause you to be a thief when you never picked up so much as a pen without permission. It can cause you to be sexually promiscuous, when you never committed fornication. Demons are real! Probably, you want to complete university before yielding to this admonition. You might be thinking 'let me enjoy it, and complete like you did'. Well, I thought I was enjoying myself, but never knew I was destroying my life, and trading away my soul. The Almighty God preserved me for reasons fully revealed to Him.

In learning institutions, social clubs are tagged negative because of the activities of the membership, which can be transformed. Banning of social clubs might help, but would not fix the trouble. It might shock you to know that even when there was a suspension, students carried out initiation processes outside campus, which was even worse, as students could easily run into lethal complications. University authorities might succeed in banning social clubs at universities and colleges in Sierra Leone. But can you ban social clubs in all universities and colleges around the globe? Colleges have regulations that govern them. Universities have regulations, and students have their rights, which could not be violated. Even if there's a universal ban, students can go to nightclubs. Students can even form off-campus social clubs, which boils down to the same thing. My objective is not just to stop those activities on campus, but to totally transform the student-domain, so that wherever students are, you see transformed personalities. Wherever they go, you should see regenerated Beings in Christ. So what they need is a **worldwide campaign** to help them understand the disadvantages of engaging in those evil practices, and the benefits of living for Christ. There are Christian universities, and colleges, around the world, but if Christians can help win authorities of non-Christian learning institutions, then the fight against inhuman social clubs would be easier. I had done this, but again I renounce membership of Quimanora Club, Cyclades Club, Diogramix Club and the Concordia Fraternity. By the Power of the Holy Ghost and in the Name of Jesus, I denounce every oath and purge my body, soul and spirit of every demonic substance related to any of those groups. I wash my total being with the Blood of Jesus.

University Officials have enormous responsibilities in their respective institutions. But for them to properly discharge their duties, they need to be qualified, well-trained and competent. Their functions are not only limited to teaching, counselling and guarding students, but should also help provide essential technical machinery to aid student-success. Well, they're not expected to physically provide funding, where applicable, but must be the drive to providing the relevant technical needs. Our Electrical Engineering laboratory, at Fourah Bay College, was dilapidated, which made it very difficult for students to carry out their respective projects or mini-projects. I had to run around town to find components, which was the case with many other students. I had to run to another college campus to implement my mechanical design. When I wanted to access the Internet, especially on research, I had to run down town to achieve that goal. How can a university reside students on campus, with no good Internet access? All those events led to fatigue and loss of time. And remember, time lost would never be regained. University Officials should try to provide accommodation for all university students as that helps them remain in their educational drive. When you reside on campus, you're supposed to focus on your academic work, and should have access to every needed educational facility on campus. So the university and other tertiary Institutions should provide good Electronic Libraries, and Laboratories, for students. Computer courses should be included into Secondary School Curricula. English Language and Mathematics should be made requirements to promote to any class in Secondary School. It's very ironic. How can English Language and Mathematics be made requirements to enter universities and not enforced in pre-Tertiary schools? So school officials should help students utilize their talents to the fullest.

Talent is the most treasured gift offered to every man by The Almighty God when travelling to this world, and he expects man to utilize it to the maximum. In Matthew 25:14-15, Scripture says, 'For the Kingdom of Heaven is as a man travelling into a far country, who called his own servants, and delivered unto them his goods. And unto one he gave five talents, to another two and unto another one; to every man according to his several 'ability...' (KJV). Similarly, this is how The Almighty God distributes talents to humanity, which defines every man's ability. He gives some multiple talents and others single. But he expects every man to utilize his talent to his peak. In Matthew 25:20, Scripture says, 'And so he that had received five talents came and brought other five talents...' The man who received the five talents multiplied his talents. He yielded fruits. He executed his assignment and his Lord said unto him, 'Well done, thou good and faithful Servants: thou hast been faithful over a few things, I will make thee ruler over many things: enter thou into the Joy of the Lord' – Matthew 25:21. But the man who received the single talent said unto his Lord, 'And I was afraid, and went and hid thy talent in the earth...' – Matthew 25:25. The man with the single talent didn't know what he had. He couldn't develop his talent. He didn't apply it. He left it dormant and handed it back to his Lord, as he gave it to him. And in Matthew 25:26, his Lord got enraged and said unto him, 'Thou wicked and slothful Servant...' That's why students need to pray for God to reveal their assignments, so that they would know what to do with their talents. When you recognize your talent and unveil your assignment, you would know your pre-ordained field of study. Because missing your talent, and assignment, can lead to delay, it can lead to failure and it can lead to misplacement. Like the man with the single talent, some know they have a talent, but are afraid to apply it. Some even know their Assignments, but due to mediocrity, they do not execute them. When you utilize your talent, as expected, The Almighty God rewards you – he elevates you, like the man with the five talents. But when you don't utilize your talent in the interest of humanity, and in the interest of Heaven, The Almighty God would rebuke and hold you accountable.

When you recognize your talent, accept and develop it. But developing your talent alone would not help, until you recognize your Assignment. Your Assignment can only be revealed by The Almighty God; that's why you need to pray. But for your prayer to be effective, you must have a healthy relationship with The Almighty God. When some of the Vagabond Jews, Exorcists, attempted to cast out evil Spirits, in the Name of Jesus, from demon-possessed humans, an evil Spirit answered, 'Jesus I know, and Paul I know; but who are ye?' (Acts 19:15). Demons recognize Spiritual Stature. They know who has The Holy Spirit, and they know who doesn't have The Holy Spirit. It is the Holy Spirit that connects you to the Trinity. You would only have a healthy relationship with the Trinity when you have The Holy Spirit. As you work in your Talent and Assignment, demonic obstructions show up.

One of the major Satanic spirits that operates in the student-domain is the spirit of witchcraft. The spirit of witchcraft held me captive for years. The spirit of witchcraft is a spirit of delay. The spirit of witchcraft is a spirit of failure. The spirit of witchcraft is a spirit of misplacement. And the spirit of witchcraft is a spirit of extermination. When they fail to delay you, when they unsuccessfully try to get you failed, when they cannot misplace you, they fight to remove you from the surface of the Earth. My parents believed in Sorcery. Many times, when complicated issues cropped up in the family, which couldn't be figured out naturally, they consulted Sorcerers to get answers. When the late Grandma Nancy died, they consulted a Sorcerer to determine the cause of her illness. When the late Sirmin died in Makeni, they consulted a Sorcerer and it was rumoured that, according to the information received, he was eaten by witches. He was not even allowed to start schooling, as he had a great future. At six months, he was doing incredible things which displayed his mental advancement. He was loved by everyone he came in contact with. But any Spiritual Investigation executed outside the Name of Jesus is of the Devil. Only Jesus can reveal Spiritual truth without a negative tag.

You cannot fight against the spirit of witchcraft when you don't have the Holy Spirit. Jesus says, 'But ye shall receive Power, after that the Holy Ghost is come upon you...' (Acts 1:8). So you only receive Power to fight against witches when you have The Holy Spirit. In 1 Corinthians 6:18-20, Paul says, '...but he that committeth Fornication sinneth against his own body. What? Know ye not that your body is the Temple of the Holy Ghost, which is in you...' Fornication, like its specialized counterpart adultery, keeps The Holy Spirit away from you. When you get into fornication, you have defiled the Temple of God. The Holy Spirit cannot reside in a filthy container, because our God is Holy. You have to be purified to house The Holy Spirit. So you only become powerful when you have The Holy Spirit. You can only defeat powers of darkness when The Holy Spirit resides in you. Remember the demon-possessed young lady I had trouble with? When she was not into fornication, she succeeded in keeping the demon, the white man, away from her through prayer. But whenever she ran into fornication, she prayed, but the demon couldn't go. Fornication almost destroyed my academic fantasy, and hence my life. The witchcraft was succeeding because I was into fornication and never knew about the Manipulation. I could've been made impotent by that demon, which would have been a long-lasting trauma. I could've been convicted of murder, if my ex-girlfriend who died had passed that night with me. That could have earned me life imprisonment or even the Death Penalty. But our Merciful God delivered me.

In the Old Testament, Exodus 22:18, Scripture says, 'Thou shalt not suffer a witch to live'. But in The New Testament, Jesus says 'Ye have heard that it hath been said, Thou shalt love thy Neighbour, and hate thine Enemy. But I say unto you, Love your Enemies' – Matthew 5:43-44. Witches are enemies of humanity. When Jesus says 'Love your Enemies', He's not talking about Satan and his demons. There's no way Jesus would instruct us to love Satan and his demons – God forbid! Jesus was talking about human enemies. He was referring to human agents of the devil. He was talking to man, as anybody who doesn't want to see you truly succeed is considered an enemy. But human-enemies are controlled by Satanic spirits. Witches are controlled by Satan's Spirit of Witchcraft. So we would love the humans and hate the Satanic Spirits. Remember, we wrestle not against Flesh and Blood (Ephesians 6:10-12). We don't fight against Flesh and Blood. We don't fight against humans. We fight against Satanic Spirits. So all we would do is pray to get them delivered. We would wrestle to kick the Witchcraft Spirits out of them, so that they would be free. No matter what these humans might have done, Jesus needs every soul He created. But as we pray, we would let them know that the Spirit of Witchcraft is a Killer of Academic Destiny. It's a killer of destiny.

If students apply The True Success Equation, then all forms of Examinations Malpractice would cease. And Lecturers/Tutors, Examiners, Invigilators, Secretaries, Office Runners, Parents/Guardians and their resident relations would support students to fight against Examinations Malpractices. A Lecturer can give a question paper to a Secretary for official reasons and she might illegally copy it to a student. A Secretary could give a question paper to an Office Runner, on official purpose, and he might illegally give it to a student. A Parent might give his child money for Bribery. An Invigilator may compromise and allow students to violate Examinations Regulations. A Lecturer's offspring might secretly pick-up Examinations questions, at home, and handover to a friend. So, all Stakeholders must be involved in the fight against Examinations Malpractice.

As a student, you can have the talent, you can apply physical effort, but if there is a Spiritual blockade, all your talent and effort would remain wasted, until spiritually addressed. Prayer is very essential in academic pursuit, but for your prayer to be very effective, you need to have a healthy relationship with our Heavenly Father, The Holy Spirit must remain your Chief Guide, and our Lord Jesus must certify you. And when you pray, believe and pray according to the Will of The Almighty God. The Almighty God says, 'Call unto me and I will answer...,' so do not wait until you become a victim – deal with it now. I wasted years at the university, because I didn't know the cause of my delay. I didn't know the cause of my temporary failures. But when it was revealed, I held on to Jesus and made Him my best Friend, because fighting alongside Jesus yields only one Result – Winning.

I Love you and God bless you – in The Name of Jesus Christ.

■■■

ADDENDUM

Other family members who supported this project
Mrs. Cecilia Nyangbe Koroma
Lt. Col. (Rtd.) Andrew F. Koroma
Haja Aminata Koroma
Mrs. Jenneh Nyorbay

Scriptural References
All Scriptures taken from King James Version of the Bible

Other References
The IQ Definition
by Alfred Binet

Definitions
Mende Tribe – Largest Ethnic Group in Sierra Leone
Ngor – Title meaning 'Elder' in Mende tribe
Kongosa – Meaning 'gossip' in Krio dialect
Non sibi, sed Aliis – "Not for self, but for others": Fourah Bay College Motto
Samou – Samuel's ethnic name, but not registered

Samuel's Major Assignment
Goal: To establish a Worldwide Writing Ministry. I shall also be engaged in Direct Training.

Writing is one of the powerful Methodologies of Evangelism. The bible we read is a Writing Assignment.

Campaign: To see man succeed on this planet, through Education, and remain Indigenes of God's Kingdom. I shall be doing Books, Articles, Songs, Movies and Direct Training.

Movies
I shall be doing movie scripts and work with the Movie Industry to get them produced. Already, I have started working on my first movie script entitled **Life as a Student.** That video would help humanity see the true picture of my first book, **Life as a Student.**

Songs
I have written at least eight songs that would be launched after recording, and other related arrangements, are complete. Some of the Songs include **King of Kings**, **Jehovah wi dae praise you, Nya longor ar bi yae** and **Oh my Jesus.**

Article to Publish - Mum
In honour of my mother, I have written an article entitled **Mum**, which shall be my first published article. And I believe that article would be meaningful, and helpful, to other mothers around the Globe. Many other articles shall be published, as I carry out my Writing Assignment.

Social Media Contribution
I have done many articles on Facebook, and minor comments on Twitter, on different issues that are helping to positively transform humanity. I am also doing commentaries on WhatsApp and Instagram.

About my next books
Already, as led by The Holy Spirit, I have started working on my next two books. Either of them shall be published first. The third would be published after the two, as indicated.

1. **Executing your Assignment**
   Every man on this planet was born to execute a specific Assignment. You can be an Engineer, you could be a Lawyer, you might be a Pastor, but the divine basics remain identical. So get ready for **Executing your Assignment**.
2. **Understanding the Strategies of Satan**
   In this end time, Satan is developing new strategies to distract, deceive and dehumanize humanity. Even the very elect might be entrapped. So our Lord Jesus is unravelling all hidden tricks of the devil, to help save mankind from eternal destruction. Watch out for **Understanding the Strategies of Satan**.
3. **Living Mathematics**
   Many students consider Mathematics a scary course. When they hear the word **Mathematics**, they get agitated. They believe Mathematics is only for a certain set of people. Yes, talents are distributed by The Almighty God, but the basics can be understood by the general populace. Watch out for **Living Mathematics!**

Education vs Assignment
Education prepares you for your Assignment. The better you can read and write, the better you can think, the better your skills, the better you can execute your Assignment.

The Need for Christian membership
To help you get deeper understanding of Christian principles, I strongly admonish you become a member of any local Church – a church headed by a pastor. Find a Church that believes in the existence of the Trinity - a Ministry that believes in the operations of the Holy Spirit. You need to mature to execute your Assignment and maintain your salvation.

Spiritual Status of the Koroma Family
Most members of the Koroma family are now Christians. By the power of the Holy Ghost, everyone would be saved - in the Name of Jesus.

Educational Status of the Koroma Family
The Koroma Family has produced graduates and post-graduates in different fields of study, and continues to do so.

■ ■ ■

www.ingramcontent.com/pod-product-compliance
Lightning Source LLC
Chambersburg PA
CBHW070953080526
44587CB00015B/2292